· A HISTORY LOVER'S ·
GUIDE TO
GALVESTON

TRISTAN SMITH

THE
History
PRESS

Published by The History Press
Charleston, SC
www.historypress.com

Front cover, top left: Galveston Seawall, Beach and Pleasure Pier. *Author's collection. Top, center*: 1900 Storm Survivor centennial marker. *Author's collection.* Bottom: Ashton Villa. *Author's collection.*
Back cover, top: The Stewart Building. *Author's collection. Bottom*: Sacred Heart Catholic Church. *Author's collection.*

First published 2024

Manufactured in the United States

ISBN 9781467156325

Library of Congress Control Number: 2023949139

For those lost in the numerous tragedies to strike Galveston.

I hope this book helps piece your stories together.

CONTENTS

Acknowledgements   7
Preface   9
Introduction   11

1. Downtown   23
   The Strand and Mechanic Streets   26
   Market and Postoffice Streets   42
   The Rest of Downtown   51
2. The Line   80
3. The Factory and Warehouse District   86
4. The East End   92
5. Silk Stockings District   113
6. Lost Bayou District   117
7. Cedar Lawn Historic District   124
8. Out West   126
   San Jacinto Neighborhood   127
   The West End   131
   Broadway Cemetery Historic District   134
9. Along the Seawall   144
   Stewart Beach   156
10. The Outskirts   162
11. Pelican Island and Beyond   173

Bibliography   187
About the Author   191

ACKNOWLEDGEMENTS

The first time that I visited Galveston Island was back around 2002. I traveled here with my wife, whose grandmother and aunt lived in Houston. After a sightseeing tour through Houston, we traveled to Galveston. I was fascinated by the stark contrast of historical preservation between the two. With so much destruction, and so much peril, facing the island community since its founding, it was amazing to me the fortitude of those living in Galveston.

Almost a decade later, we moved to Houston. Visits to the island became more frequent but focused more on the beach and places like Moody Gardens, places to take your kids. While focused less on places like Gaido's and historical districts like the Strand and the East End, I got to see a different slice of Galveston's history: the playground aspect of the island's story. I saw a different contrast, that between the historic commercial district, a burgeoning residential community and a thriving vacation destination.

Native lands, conquistadors, pirates, revolutionaries, rebels, entrepreneurs, millionaires, prizefighters, prostitutes, madams, Texas Republic leaders, immigrants and moguls have all called Galveston home. Here you find the heart of what brought Texas to the forefront of American history. Explore the Line, historic residential neighborhoods, the Seawall and historic districts like the Strand and the East End, as well as places you might not think to explore. Sites from the Civil War and from the largest and most destructive natural disaster to hit the United States in its history, a thriving red-light district and Prohibition-repellant speakeasys still remain—if you know where to look.

I continue to find fascinating the different layers of the island's history and, much like in *A History Lover's Guide to Houston*, I wanted to invite people to explore. I've included the easy-to-explore places, like museums, historical sites, parks, retail shops, restaurants and cafés. I've also placed here private residences, closed attractions, private businesses and shuttered establishments. Especially in these latter locations, please respect the boundaries of admission and decorum. Photographs and passersby at these places are generally taken in stride and, often, are expected. Just visit with the utmost respect.

I hope that you will enjoy reading and utilizing this book as much as I have enjoyed researching and writing it. I could not have completed this book without the assistance, guidance and support of so many other people. I would like to thank my editor, Ben Gibson, at The History Press for believing in not only this publication but also two other books we have worked together on. To The History Press and the Arcadia Publishing team for bringing this book from a hodgepodge of notes, pictures and site names to the book you see before you—thank you so very much.

To the people of Galveston: residents, business owners, BOI (born on the island) or IBC (islander by choice), thank you for opening your island, your beaches and your sites to those passing through. The island is an amazing and special place even beyond the sand castles and seafood. Thank you more specifically to Marisa Morales at Miller's Seafood, the staff at the Galveston Bookshop, Eric Broussard at the Bryan Museum, Pat Welsh at the Moody Mansion, Jodi Wright-Gidley at the Galveston County Museum and Dwayne Jones at the Galveston Historical Foundation (and all of their staff members) for additional assistance.

And, last but not least, to my people. Sara, thank you for being my travel companion, test reader and photo assistant and for giving me space to write (and thanks to Amelia, Violet, Benjamin and Cheryl for sharing her with me)—I love you. To Antoinette and Jeremy, thanks for indulging my trips with Theo and Max so they could help me explore the island even more. To Theo and Max, for ungrudgingly (usually) agreeing to join me on my explorations. To my mom and dad, thank you for instilling in me my sense of adventure. I write now because of these adventures: I can't not do it. Thank you, everyone.

PREFACE

If you want to write a book about historic places in Texas, there are numerous places to delve into and explore. I've explored numerous cities, large and small, throughout the state, and many of them fascinate me, causing me to return time and again (I'm looking at you, San Antonio and the area surrounding Goliad). However, one place that sits close to home is Galveston Island. I moved to Houston, Texas, from Lawrence, Kansas. While Lawrence is close to Kansas City, moving to Houston was a bit of a shock—much larger, much more time to get around, with tons of sites to see and places to explore.

When we moved to Houston, one of our early forays out and about was to Galveston. How could you not visit the island's beaches when you live so close in Houston? Once there, I was amazed by how well the city has preserved its past—not an easy task when massive storms blow through occasionally. For decades, efforts by city movers and shakers, especially helped by the vision of the Galveston Historical Foundation, have helped save scores of buildings throughout the island, if not hundreds.

There is no way that I can do justice to every single historic structure in Galveston. However, there are a bevy of books, websites and other projects that have covered just about everything in Galveston's history. There's more to uncover, though. I think the emergence of the African American diaspora on the island, with a deep and long heritage to be told, will start filling in those gaps in the decade to come.

Galveston is an exciting place to explore. Whether you want to see the beaches, the nature reserves, the tourist spots or the historic sites, there is no shortage of places to visit. You can return time and again to the island and see multiple aspects every time. Unlike so many other tourist locales, there is no real ideal time to visit. There is the beach in the summer, Dickens on the Strand around the holidays, historic home tours in the spring, Oktoberfest and other festivals throughout the fall and, in the late fall or early spring, you have one of the most festive Mardi Gras celebrations outside of New Orleans. The museums, historic sites and so much more are open throughout the year.

I encourage you to stray from the Strand and explore the rest of downtown. Leave the beach and walk some of the Seawall. Explore the neighborhoods, see the sights that most people pass right by. There's so much to see on this relatively small island. I've explored this island, and I don't know if I could fit everything in two or three books, let alone this one title. Have fun exploring. I hope you enjoy Galveston.

INTRODUCTION

While the first European settlements established on what is now Galveston Island were constructed around 1816, the land was originally inhabited by members of the Karankawa and Akokisa tribes, who called the island Auiai. Galveston has a storied past that counts conquistadors and European explorers among pirates and organized criminals, as well as Texas founding fathers. What was once fertile ground for island natives for one reason became fertile ground for entrepreneurs for others.

Shortly after Alonso Álvarez de Pineda's expedition sailed past the island in 1519, heading from Florida to the Panuco River, Spain laid claim to the entire Gulf Coast; including Galveston Island. Less than a decade later, in November 1528, Cabeza de Vaca and his crew found themselves shipwrecked on or near the island, calling it the Isle of Doom, or Isla de Malhado, before setting out on their trek into Mexico. Over the next century, the island received many names from a slew of explorers, including Isla Blanca, or the White Island, and later Isla de Aranjuez or simply Aranjuez Island. One of its longest-serving names, outside of Galveston, was San Luis (from Saint Louis, as it was named by French explorer La Salle in 1685).

Early maps indicate a few other names the island has gone by. The earliest known map of the island dates to 1721, created by French explorer Bénard de la Harpe, who named the bay Port Francois; the island remained unnamed. Then, in 1785, the Spanish explorer José de Evia, while charting the Gulf Coast, named the island San Luis but named the bay in honor of Bernardo de Gálvez y Madrid, the Count of Gálvez, referring to it as Bahia

Bernardo de Gálvez was a Spanish military leader and government official who served as governor of Spanish Louisiana and Cuba and later as viceroy of New Spain. The celebrated soldier helped support the colonists and French allies during the Revolutionary War. His efforts are behind the naming of the island after him. *Courtesy of the Library of Congress.*

de Galvestowm or Galvestowm Bay. His name for the island continued to be used for a number of years, especially by the Spanish and the Mexicans and even as late as by Stephen F. Austin's colony. The name, San Luis, continues to be used to this day for the pass at the west end of the island.

Pirates arrived next, establishing the first permanent European settlements. Around 1816, Louis-Michel Aury, a French privateer operating in the Gulf, started using the island as his base of operations in Mexico's rebellion against Spain. However, the following year, after returning from a failed raid against Spain, Aury found that fellow pirate Jean Lafitte had taken up residence on the island. Having been driven from the coast of New Orleans, Lafitte settled on the island, naming it Campeche and appointing himself the "head of government" for his new pirate kingdom. He and his pirates remained on the island until 1821. Then the United States Navy arrived with an ultimatum: leave or die. Lafitte chose the former but burned Campeche to the ground, sailing out under cover of darkness.

When the Mexican War for Independence came to a close, the new congress of Mexico issued a proclamation that established the Port of Galveston. Five years later, in 1830, Mexico erected a customs house on the island. During the Texas Revolution, Galveston served as the main port of the Texas navy. Galveston also served as its capital when, in 1836, the seat of government was moved to the island from nearby Harrisburg by interim president David G. Burnet. That same year, Michel B. Menard, with several other partners, purchased just over 4,600 acres from the Austin Colony to found what would become Galveston. Surveys of the new town were completed in 1837, and a city plan was designed by Gail Borden. Sales took off in 1838, and by 1839, enough work had been accomplished to adopt a charter and gain incorporation by the Congress of the Republic of Texas. Along with the rest of the republic, when Texas joined the Union in 1845, Galveston came along for the ride.

With prosperity sometimes comes blemishes as well. The City of Galveston, in antebellum Texas, was a significant port of activity in the slave trade, becoming the largest slave market west of New Orleans. Secession eventually led Texas, and Galveston, to the Confederacy; the state departed the Union in 1861. While Galveston was touched a few times by the war, it was on January 1, 1863, that it saw its greatest role during the conflict. Confederate forces under Major General John B. Magruder attacked and expelled occupying Union troops from the city during the Battle of Galveston. From that point until the end of the war, Galveston remained in rebel hands. Then, in May 1865, the *Lark* deftly avoided the Union blockade of the

Left: This portrait is said to be of the famed pirate Jean Lafitte, painted in the early nineteenth century by an unknown artist. Historic sites associated with Lafitte can be found along the Gulf Coast, including the site of his house Maison Rouge and the possible location of his Galveston village, which he named Campeche, denoted by a historical marker. *Courtesy of Rosenberg Library, Galveston.*

Right: David Burnet, seen here in a mid-1800s photograph, was president of the interim government of the Republic of Texas during 1836 and again in 1841. He also served as the republic's vice president from 1839 to 1841 and as secretary of state for the newly admitted state of Texas in 1846. *Courtesy of the Center for American History, University of Texas at Austin.*

harbor and headed for Havana, the last Confederate ship to slip through any of the Southern port blockades. Following the end of the war, work still needed to be done. On June 19, 1865, Union general Gordon Granger and his troops arrived on the island. During his occupation, he officially read out the Emancipation Proclamation, issued in 1863, that declared all enslaved people were free. That date is now the federal holiday Juneteenth.

During the mid-nineteenth century, Galveston would emerge as an international city. Bustling with the activity of immigration and trade from throughout the United States and the world, Galveston was Texas's largest and most important city, as well as its prime commercial center. Throughout the latter part of the nineteenth century, Galveston was one of the nation's busiest ports and the world's leading port for cotton experts. Railroads began entering and leaving the island by the new causeway linking the island with mainland Texas. In addition, churches, schools, gaslights, hospitals, an opera house, an orphanage and the state's first medical college and school for nurses were all established during this period. Called the Ellis Island of the West, the island was also the primary point of entry for European immigrants settling in the western United States. German immigration was so common at the time that German was commonly used on the streets and can still be found in references to this day. However, the immigrants of the time were not all poor, like is seen in the movies. Yes, some were, but there were many educated middle-class individuals and families among those seeking refuge.

Additionally, Reconstruction served as a high point on the island in regard to civil rights for African Americans. Leaders such as George Ruby and Norris Wright Cuney would emerge, working to establish education and employment opportunities for Black people and organize Black voters to support the Republican Party. This led to higher employment and higher wages for Black people in Galveston, while it led Cuney to the chairmanship of the Texas Republican Party, the most powerful position held by any Black American in that era.

Unfortunately, this growth and success came to a screeching halt in the early morning on September 8, 1900. Continuing to hold the record as the United States' deadliest natural disaster, the 1900 Storm swept in, and by noon, low-lying areas near the gulf and bay sides of the city were flooding with increased winds. A fifteen-foot high storm surge slammed the island near four o'clock that afternoon, with wind speeds estimated at 125 miles an hour by U.S. Weather Bureau chief meteorologist Isaac Cline. The aftermath was brutal and devastating. An estimated six to twelve thousand people were killed in the storm, many more were missing and much of the island was laid to ruin. Following the storm, with many having preceded it and a healthy fear of those that might follow, city leaders decided to take action. A permanent concrete seawall along a long stretch of beachfront was constructed to hold back higher surf. In building it, engineers also had to raise the entire grade of the city some seventeen feet on the other side of the wall to several feet nearer the bay. The entire project took from 1902 to 1910 to complete.

The aftermath of the 1900 Storm was devastating for Galveston. Attempts were made to draw new investment to the city with little luck. Many people, and companies, decided to flee the island following the storm. Additionally, development was complicated due to the construction of the Houston Ship Channel, bringing the Port of Galveston into direct competition with the

This 1871 bird's-eye view of Galveston was created by Camille Drie. Highlighted sites on the map include the island's civic and religious institutions along with several packets and ships in the harbor. *Courtesy of the Center for American History, University of Texas at Austin.*

The 1900 Storm is the deadliest natural disaster in United States history. In its wake, it left between six and twelve thousand fatalities, with ten thousand people homeless in a city of fewer than thirty-eight thousand. Most deaths occurred in and near Galveston, after the storm surge inundated the coastline and city with eight to twelve feet of water. This image portrays the aftermath of such destruction, with bodies being hauled from the wreckage. *Courtesy of the Library of Congress.*

Port of Houston. To help rebuild the population of the island, Galveston actively sought out immigration through a plan called the Galveston Movement; nearly ten thousand immigrants came to the island between 1907 and 1914. While these methods helped, Galveston could not keep up with the explosion of development happening at Houston, on the mainland.

William Moody Jr. helped to diversify the island's traditional port-related industries, and the military helped as well. The Coastal Artillery—being built by the U.S. Army and halted by the hurricane—was finished in the

The ten-mile-long seawall in Galveston was constructed following the 1900 Storm to help protect the island and its inhabitants. While it performed as intended, passive erosion changed the way the beach and area once looked. The waves seen here—during the August 1915 hurricane, which drew comparisons to the 1900 Storm—crashed against the seawall, which mitigated a similar-scale disaster. *Courtesy of the Special Collections, University of Houston Libraries.*

early 1900s, opening in 1903 as Fort Crockett. The Galveston-Houston Electric Railway was established in 1911 between Galveston and Houston, the fastest rail line in 1925 and 1926. This, and the construction of the seawall, actually helped the city reemerge in the 1920s and 1930s as a tourist destination.

Exploiting the prohibition of liquor and gambling, figures such as Oscar "Dutch" Voigt and brothers Sam and Rosario Maceo emerged, offering entertainment at such places as the Balinese Room to wealthy Houstonians and other travelers. Through the gambling combined with the prostitution on the island, Galveston came back to prominence in a completely different manner than before the storm. Galvestonians not only accepted the illegal activities but helped with support, referring to their island as the Free State of Galveston.

Just like during the First World War, the island became a hotbed of activity again during World War II. The Galveston Municipal Airport, predecessor to Scholes International Airport, was redesignated a U.S. Army Air Corp base called Galveston Army Air Field. That, along with fortifications at Fort Crockett, Fort Travis and Fort San Jacinto, has given the island and the coast a strong barrier of defense. It was also during this time that the Moody

Grand hotels and resorts have long been a common sight along the beachfront. The Beach Hotel, once located on the beach between Tremont and Twenty-Fourth Streets, was constructed in 1882–83 and destroyed by fire in 1898. *Courtesy of the Rosenberg Library, Galveston.*

family, under William Moody Jr. and his wife, Libbie Shearn Rice Moody, established their foundation that would go on to help strengthen the cultural and social foundation of the island for years to come.

Following the war, the military reduced its presence on the island, which led to an increase in police enforcement. Frustrated with local officiating, the Texas Rangers began a massive campaign of raids on the island and eventually closed the door to the Open Era of Galveston. As a result, the tourism industry crashed, and so did the rest of Galveston. The culture and the economy of the island, despite a resurgence in the late twentieth century, has yet to recover to those levels. However, the diversified economy established after the 1900 Storm allowed Galveston to weather this storm as well.

The Galveston Historical Foundation began efforts to preserve the city's historic buildings as early as 1957. Places like the Strand Historic District began to emerge, as did a more family friendly tourism movement on the island. Also, Texas A&M University at Galveston and Galveston Community College joined the University of Texas Medical Branch. The island's tourism, education and commercial endeavors began to add up—and shore up Galveston's resources. The city managed, despite heavy damage, to survive Hurricanes Carla and Ike, in 1961 and 2008, respectively.

Ike, however, laid waste to the island like it hadn't seen since the 1900 Storm. The storm surge came in at about fourteen feet, moving around the famed Galveston Seawall and flooding the streets as the winds knocked down homes, businesses and the famed Balinese Room. Because of the destruction of the storm, another civil engineering feat has been suggested for the island's protection. Much like the seawall, the so-called Ike Dike would protect Galveston and the bay. Since 2009, it has inched closer and closer to realization, in hopes that it will protect the island and its resources for another century and longer.

Chapter 1

DOWNTOWN

Officially called Avenue B in early maps and in the original plat of Galveston, the name Strand came from a German immigrant named Michael William Shaw. The businessman, who opened a jewelry store on the corner of Avenue B and Twenty-Third Street, did not like the name "Ave. B" and changed the name of the street on his stationery to "Strand." His thinking was that the street, named after one in London, would reflect a higher-class operation for his store.

Later, Shaw managed to convince other store owners on the street to change as well, and it stuck. The Strand's earliest buildings were typically constructed of wood. Unfortunately, this meant that they were susceptible to fires and the storms that frequently crashed against the island. Eventually, those early structures were replaced with iron-fronted buildings, ones that might withstand such destruction. Even the two oldest buildings on the Strand date to only 1855 and 1858, and most other historic buildings primarily date to the 1870s and 1880s. As the port city of Galveston boomed throughout the nineteenth century, the Strand also became the region's main business center. It was so popular and well known that it was known, for a time, as the Wall Street of the South.

The Strand and the surrounding downtown area became an extremely popular place for major business due to immigration and the Port of Galveston vessel traffic. Included among these businesses were the state's five largest banks, wholesalers, cotton brokers, attorneys, slave auctioneers,

Above: This image, taken in 1912, shows the hustle and bustle of Galveston's docks. The Port of Galveston was established by the Congress of Mexico in October 1825, when this land was still part of Mexico. It is the oldest port in the Gulf of Mexico west of New Orleans. By World War I, Galveston was a leading port in the world and had become a major immigration center. *Courtesy of Southern Methodist University, Central University Libraries, DeGolyer Library.*

Right: The Isidore Leclere Building was originally an office for a coal yard and is one of the oldest buildings on the Strand. Right at the top of the door, you can see a common marker on the island, a Hurricane Ike high-water mark that shows the level from the September 13, 2008 storm. *Author's collection.*

and commission merchants, among others. Between 1838 and 1842, eighteen newspapers were started (although only the *Galveston News*, founded in 1842, remains).

The district, however, suffered during several Civil War battles, primarily due to its proximity to the harbor. The Union barricaded the city when it overtook Galveston, and during the Battle of Galveston, the returning Confederates fought from nearly every corner of the region. Several buildings suffered damage from shots and from shelling. Warfare caused many of the businesses to close, moving to Houston until the war's end. The prosperity returned following the war.

Unfortunately, downtown's prosperity would come to an abrupt end in 1900. That September, when a major hurricane blew in, devastating much of the city, the Strand and the surrounding district suffered mightily. Many buildings sustained catastrophic damage; some lost entire floors, while others lost only minor architectural flourishes and details. Due to the catastrophic nature of the damage, many businesses elected to move away from the wharf, some away from the district, and even others off the island entirely. The area essentially became a warehouse district for the early part of the twentieth century, only seeing its revival in the 1960s when the Junior League of Galveston County stepped in to restore two buildings—a process that gathered even more steam when, in 1973, the Galveston Historical Foundation created a trust fund for restoration projects within the district. That spurred a revitalization project that is ongoing to this day. Despite this, in 2008, Hurricane Ike struck the island, leaving behind significant damage to the Strand district, as well as across the island. As a result, in 2009, the National Trust for Historic Preservation added the district to that year's list of America's Most Endangered Places.

Today the entire district, anchored by the Strand, features shops, restaurants, bars, museums, art galleries and nightclubs. It is the location of one of the largest Mardi Gras celebrations in the country and of the Christmas festival called Dickens on the Strand. One of the newest features is the centrally located Saengerfest Park, a small square park located at Strand and Tremont that was created in the early 1990s. Look for markers denoting buildings that survived the 1900 Storm as well as high-water marks for Hurricane Ike in order to get a true picture of just how much water washed through the streets of Galveston.

THE STRAND AND MECHANIC STREETS

Ball, Hutchings & Company
John Sealy Office Building/Riondo's Ristorante
2326–2328 Strand Street

Designed in 1895 by Nicholas Clayton, the Ball, Hutchings & Co. building replaced the original J.S. Brown Hardware Building, which owned this and adjacent sites to the west prior to the 1877 fire. Standing at two stories and constructed of gray and pink granite, red Texas sandstone and buff-colored terra-cotta, it was constructed for George Ball, John Henry Hutchings and John Sealy. Following four decades of joint partnership, they hired Clayton to design a new building to house their entire commission and banking operation. It was built as two individual buildings that were connected. The Renaissance Revival–style structure features rusticated stone arches at the entryways with terra-cotta detailing. The corner building features the name "Hutchings" on its entablature while, next door, "Sealy" is featured. The combined buildings also sport a Lone Star medallion on panels of the entablature, with the dates 1854 (the founding of the partnership), and 1895 (the construction of the building).

When the Federal blockade closed the port of Galveston during the Civil War, the firm moved to Houston for its duration, carrying on its trade in cotton to help the Confederate cause. Following the war, in 1867, George Sealy, younger brother of John, was made a partner in the firm. Later mergers, in 1930 and 1958, led to the name change to First Hutchings-Sealy National Bank of Galveston. Following a move to the Rosenberg Bank at Twenty-Second and Market Streets, a new building for the bank was constructed in 1956 and again in 1972. Inside the original 1895 building, American Indemnity Company was founded in 1913, remaining until 1958. Following Hurricane Carla, Ursuline Academy moved in and held classes there for several years after the storm severely damaged its own building. The landmark building underwent restoration in 1985.

La King's Confectionery
2317–2323 Strand Street

Jimmy King began making candy in Houston in the 1920s, learning the trade from Old World candy makers. Nearly fifty years later, in 1976, Jimmy's oldest son, Jack, moved his family to the Strand. His goal was to re-create an old-fashioned confectionery, using the nineteenth-century formulas and methods handed down to him by Jimmy and traditional equipment and procedures to make his goods.

Walking in, you ascend the steps, walk across the creaky wood floors and find a veritable Willy Wonka–esque spread of sugary goods. La King's features a working 1920s soda fountain and vintage saltwater taffy-pulling equipment while also making and serving Purity ice cream. Founded in 1889 in Galveston, Purity was Texas's first ice cream manufacturer.

Thomas Jefferson League Building
2301–2307 Strand Street

After robbing Cohn Brothers clothing store in 1869, thieves set a fire to cover their tracks, which resulted in a mile-wide swath of the Strand being consumed. In 1871, Thomas Jefferson League began construction on this building. League was the son of a prominent pioneer family and served as an attorney, later becoming a judge. Working with local craftsmen, League erected this commercial building sporting a decorative cast-iron first-floor façade with a galvanized iron cornice.

Three stores were housed in the three-story building: Woston, Wells & Vidor, a cotton factor and commission merchant; Robinson Company, a stationer and bookseller; and Isaac Bernstein & Company, a leading clothier. Later tenants included insurance agents, clothing manufacturers and attorneys, including J.C. League, Thomas Jefferson League's brother and, at that time, owner of the building, who listed himself simply as "Capitalist." In 1921, Ben Sass and Aaron P. Levy bought this property, purchased Ben Blum Hardware Co. and moved that business into the property in 1923, where it remained for fifty years. Following the deaths of Levy and Sass in 1929 and 1935, respectively, the building and the business were purchased by Joseph Levy Rosenfield and other Levy family members, who remained owners until 1973, when Galveston Historical Foundation purchased the building. In 1979, it was listed as a Recorded Texas Historic Landmark. Today, Mercantile on the Strand is housed inside.

Old Galveston Square
2211–2223 Strand Street

As early as 1839, this location was a hub of activity. Located between two wharves and close to the Customs House, the site was ideal for business. Found here over the years were retail and wholesale merchants, insurance companies, attorneys, newspapers, restaurants, saloons and cotton factories. Old Galveston Square, presently, is composed of one contemporary structure and four historic buildings.

Located at the eastern end of the row is the E.S. Wood Building. Completed in 1857, it was part of a continuous façade formed by a row of buildings lining the entire block. Those buildings surviving today were constructed as replacements to buildings lost in the February 1870 fire. The Wood Building was partially damaged, requiring extensive repairs, but it continued to stand. The additional buildings—T.W. House, Henry Runge and the John Berlocher Buildings—were completed in 1871.

Old Galveston Square may have historically been the most ideal location for early Galveston businesses. Retail and wholesale merchants operated here as early as 1839. Today it is composed of four historic structures and one contemporary. The oldest is the 1857 E.S. Wood Building, at the eastern end of the row, while the rest were completed in 1871. *Author's collection.*

In 1904, the buildings that make up this commercial row were incorporated into one single business house by Blum Hardware. Following that, two long-term tenants were the Black Hardware Company, which occupied the building from 1917 to 1966, and Flood & Calvert, ship chandlers, which housed operations here from 1966 to 1982. In 1982, a developer purchased the property and began an extensive redevelopment that included many contemporary upgrades inside and a glass conservatory and a large sculpture located on the west side of the building. George and Cynthia Mitchell purchased the property in 1987 and continued the historic restoration of the vintage buildings. Additional, and more extensive, work was done following damage from Hurricane Ike.

Nia Cultural Center
2217 Strand Street, Suite 101

This location continues to serve Galveston as a shopping destination on the Strand. One site you should consider popping in to see is the Nia Cultural Center, the art gallery of the Juneteenth Legacy Project Headquarters. In addition to the five-thousand-square-foot mural chronicling Emancipation on the eastern exterior of the building, inside, the gallery offers a journey through African American history from the 1800s to the present featuring sculptures and paintings by local African American artists, plus a reflection area.

W.L. Moody Building
2202–2206 Strand Street

The William L. Moody Building has stood on the Strand for more than 130 years. It replaced a larger building that had been destroyed by a fire in 1882. When originally constructed, it stood at four stories; however, the 1900 Storm knocked down a decorative cornice that topped the building—along with the entire top floor. The building was constructed in 1883 to be used for cotton and banking operations for the Moody businesses. Following the storm, the original architect, Nicholas J. Clayton, repaired the structure but never replaced the top floor. You can still see Clayton's fine design work in the lower floor, decorated with cast-iron columns with brick and terra-cotta façades. For forty-two years, until closing in 2014, the building housed the beloved Colonel Bubbies military surplus store, operated by the Reiswerg family. This was Galveston's longest-running business with a single owner on the Strand when it closed. Today, the Moody building houses a retail shop with residential lofts above.

First National Bank Building/Galveston Arts Center
2127 Strand Street

The original First National Bank of Galveston Building, erected on this site in 1867, was destroyed by the 1877 fire. Constructed in its place, and almost identical in design, is this newer iteration. Standing one story short of its predecessor, this two-story brick and cast-iron structure was a near replica, even down to the salvaged and reused cast-iron hood moulds and Strand street front. Throughout the latter half of the nineteenth century, the First National Bank of Galveston was considered the most substantial bank in the state of Texas. It remained in continuous operation until 1955, when it merged with the Hutchings-Sealy Bank.

Following the merger, this building sat mostly vacant for years until the Junior League purchased and restored it. The Junior League intended it to house the Centre on the Strand, whose purpose was to promote Galveston's cultural and educational environment. This pilot project spurred the ongoing preservation and restoration for the Strand and, beyond that, the island. In 1972, the Galveston County Cultural Arts Council, now the Galveston Arts Center (GAC), opened a gallery in the building, bringing arts center classes and workshops to the community as well. That was disrupted when Hurricane Ike hit the island in 2008 and the building incurred damage. GAC moved temporarily while the building was restored, a project completed in 2015.

Nichols Building
2025 Strand Street

The Nichols Building was constructed by commission merchant Ebenezer B. Nichols in 1860 and continues to stand as one of the oldest commercial houses on the Strand. It was built at a time when brick commercial buildings were beginning to replace Galveston's original wood commercial buildings. If you can catch a glimpse of the Nichols Building's rear façade, you will see the dark red brick that is characteristic of buildings of the era and, midway up, a change in color from the original red to a more modern yellow hue, suggesting that a reconstruction of the building's upper portion had taken place.

Nichols entered into partnership with William R. Rice. Born and schooled in New York, Rice traveled to Texas with lumber in 1838, turning his attention to fighting with the Texas Rifles on the frontier before settling in Houston. With money from speculation in pecans, he entered into business with Nichols as Rice & Nichols, dealers in dry goods, groceries, hardware, crockery and similar at wholesale and retail. After acquiring interests in Galveston, Nichols moved there in 1850, becoming an officer in the Galveston Brazos Navigation Company, which drew from Houston, and began his own operations on the island. Following his service to the Confederacy, his interests on the island was notable. He organized the Bank of Galveston, dealt in real estate, was president of the Galveston City Company and helped form the Galveston Gas Company, the Galveston Wharf Company, the Texas Ice and Cold Storage Company and the Galveston, Houston and Henderson Railroad. Additionally, he was a founder of Galveston's Trinity Episcopal Church and served as grant master of the Masonic lodge of Texas before his death in late 1872.

Hendley Buildings
2002–2016 Strand Street

The Hendley Buildings, also known as Hendley Row, was constructed for brothers William and Joseph Hendley, cotton and commission merchants, between 1855 and 1859, at a time when Twentieth Street was considered the center line of Galveston. Designed in the Greek Revival style, the Hendley is the oldest brick structure on the Strand. Standing back, one can see that the building is actually four separate units that are divided by granite blocks. Come closer and you will see that on those dividing blocks, the original building owners had their initials carved right into the granite. As Koons Wharf was rapidly expanding at the time, this building was constructed to help facilitate that expansion; it was used as a shipping line headquarters between Galveston and New York City.

Shortly after the building's construction, the Civil War began, and the Hendley played a significant role in the conflict's 1863 Battle of Galveston. Confederate general John Bankhead Magruder used the Hendley building, as well as other smaller buildings on Twentieth Street, during the battle—which turned out to be short, as the Union navy was unprepared, and the

Confederacy reclaimed the island. Shell damage from this battle can still be purportedly seen on the building's exterior at the Twentieth Street–facing wall. Following the war, offices in the building were occupied by the Army Corps of Engineers until 1888. Since then, the building has served as home to offices and retail establishments, private residences, restaurants and liquor and produce operations as well as headquarters of the Galveston Historical Foundation.

U.S. Custom House/Galveston Immigration Station
1700 Strand Street

Designed in a streamlined Spanish style by New York City architect William L. Bottomley and partners, the U.S. Custom House was constructed in 1933. The three-story, tile-roofed building is raised a full story above grade and landscaped with palm trees. At the time, this elevation was more common to residential architecture than institutional buildings, but this only indicates the island's known vulnerability to flooding.

While not considered a large city in the mid-nineteenth century, Galveston emerged as an international city with immigration and trade around the United States and the world. Sometimes called the Ellis Island of the West, Galveston and its immigration centers, one of which is shown here, became the primary point of entry for European immigrants during the Victorian period. *Author's collection.*

Originally, this building grew out of need. Galveston had been the port of entry for thousands of immigrants settling not only in Texas but throughout the Southwest. When federal laws were enacted in 1875, they ended unrestricted entry of immigrants into the country, leading to the establishment of the area's first immigration station, located at Pier 29 on the island. Officials there would conduct medical exams, baggage inspections and formal processing of immigrants. In 1906, Congress chose Galveston over New Orleans as the site of major new Federal immigration station plans. While these plans were never fully realized, they called for an impressive landing station to be located on Pelican Island that would rival New York's Ellis Island.

A scaled-down station, fully operational by 1913, was promptly damaged in a 1915 hurricane and then closed altogether and relocated in 1916. The result of this path of destruction was this building, a new three-story immigration station. Inside, it contained immigration offices, dormitories, medical facilities, recreational areas and a kitchen and dining room. It was completed in 1933 and used as an immigration and deportee-staging facility until 1940, when it was converted for use as a United States customs office.

Clarke and Courts Building
2402–2406 Mechanic Street

In business for over a century in Texas, Clark and Courts Printing was headquartered in Galveston. Until the 1930s, this business was the largest printing and lithography company in the region, producing forms for state and local governments throughout Texas. In addition to wedding invites, stationery and blank books for businesses, banks and railroads, the company also sold office furniture.

The company itself was organized at Galveston by Miles Strickland in 1857. He moved the printing press to Houston during the Civil War, returned to the island afterward and hired expert printer Samuel Burke, asking him to become a partner in the business. In 1870, Robert Clark purchased Burke's interest in the firm. Less than a decade later, George M. Courts purchased Strickland's interest. The two men, George M. Courts and Robert Clarke, formed their own partnership in 1879; Clark managed the printing aspects, with Courts supervising the rest. The duo incorporated in 1887, following the company's blue-ribbon win at the State Fair of Texas for its products. By 1890, the firm had completed this office building, known as the Texas

Clarke and Courts were stationers and printers located on Tremont Street. Their operation—with headquarters in Galveston, seen here—was in business in Texas for over one hundred years. Until the 1930s, it was the largest printing and lithography company in the region. The unique sign remains for its new life as apartment lofts. *Author's collection.*

House, designed by Nicholas J. Clayton, as well as a plant and warehouse. This was Clayton's tallest commercial building, standing at five stories that housed the company's building and production plant.

Despite suffering damage during the 1900 Storm—which, incidentally, killed the company's head bookkeeper—the firm managed to print the island's first newspapers following the disastrous storm. With a focus on staying ahead of the competition, it installed the first offset press west of the Mississippi in 1907 and eventually offered customers an array of services from printing and stereotyping to bookbinding and box manufacturing. The company renewed its charter in 1936, moving its headquarters to Houston but extending its services to customers outside of Texas in Louisiana, Oklahoma, New Mexico, Arkansas, Mexico and Cuba. By 1976, the company's plants were located in Galveston, Houston and Harlingen, but it faced growing computerization advancement from its competitors. Eventually, Clark and Courts closed up shop in 1989. In 1994, the city converted the building, which today serves as a residential loft building known as Strand Lofts.

Tremont House
2300 Mechanic Street

This Tremont House is not the first in Galveston. In fact, three entities have carried the name. The first Tremont House was constructed in 1839 and was located at the corner of Postoffice and Tremont Streets before being destroyed by fire in 1865. The second Tremont Hotel was completed in 1872. This iteration fell into disrepair in the early 1900s and was, as a result, demolished in 1928. The final, and current, Tremont Hotel actually occupies the 1879 Leon and H. Blum Building, styled to recreate the atmosphere of its namesake.

This building was constructed for the cousins Leon and Human Blum and Leon's brother Sylvain. They had moved to Texas in the 1850s and, finally, to Galveston to open a dry goods wholesale and mercantile house. Leon & H. Blum would become one of the largest wholesalers in the state in the 1870s and 1880s. The firm acquired this site following the destruction of their original building during the fire of 1877. In 1879, they hired Eugene Heiner to design this three-story brick and stucco building. They rehired Heiner in 1882 to expand the building farther east along Mechanic, creating the most extensive street frontage of any of the downtown Galveston wholesale houses.

Following the Panic of 1893, the firm went bankrupt and closed up shop. In 1981, Cynthia and George Mitchell bought the Blum Building, now in a dilapidated condition but still in relatively good shape. The exterior was restored and the inside was transformed into a 124-room hotel, the first major one in downtown Galveston in nearly sixty years. During the process, the project garnered support from the National Park Service to add a fourth floor to the historic building—in the form of a mansard-roofed attic that was never realized from the original plans.

John Berlocher Buildings
2309–2315 Mechanic Street

This is an interesting little stretch of buildings. Located on the east side of the row stands the 1858–59 John Berlocher Building. Berlocher was a Swiss immigrant and commission merchant who was active in improving Galveston's downtown real estate during the 1850s–70s. This row of three 3-story brick buildings was constructed by builder John Brown for John

Berlocher. The first, and easternmost, building which is located at 2309, was erected in 1858, with the western building built soon after.

Designed in the Greek Revival style, the red brick buildings sported finely detailed sills, labels and cast-iron lintels. Berlocher ended up building four of the first brick commercial buildings in the city. Three of these were on the Strand, all on the same site and all destroyed by successive fires. Additionally, during the Battle of Galveston, his building was in the line of fire from the eleven-inch guns on the Federal *Owasco* and was damaged as a result by cannon fire. After the battle, the building was occupied by the Confederate army as a guardhouse. Unfortunately for Berlocher, these disasters, one following another, ruined his business.

In 1876, Berlocher sold this row of buildings to Gustave Opperman. It remained in the Opperman family until it was sold in 1903 to Mistrot Brothers and Company, a wholesale and retail dry goods and clothing firm. Over the years, a drugstore, a potter, the IRS, a feed store, a dance studio and a variety of retail establishments have operated out of this building. Two of the longest-running businesses included Neidermann's Galveston Builders Supply Company, located in the west building from 1923 to 1943, which was followed by J.A. Neidermann's antique store until 1979. A fire in 1980 damaged the upper floors and roof of the west building. Since then, it has undergone extensive renovations.

The Washington Building
2222–2228 Mechanic Street

Today housing the Galveston Chamber of Commerce's Visitor Information Center on the ground floor, the Washington Building was originally erected in 1873 as a sixty-room hotel called the Cosmopolitan. Following a devastating fire in 1877 that destroyed the city's Washington Hotel, a beloved city landmark, this hotel was renamed the Washington in its honor. Designed in the late Greek Revival style, it features a marble-like exterior, large French doors and fanlight transom windows allowing natural light in abundance. Its all-white exterior clearly sets the building apart from its neighbors. Additional entities housed here include the Harris and Eliza Kempner Fund on the second floor along with Mitchell Historic Properties, while the third floor features executive suites with waiting areas, a kitchen and a conference room.

J.P. Davie Building
2220 Mechanic Street

John Parker Davie, a native of Wales, was one of Galveston's pioneer businessmen. By trade, David was a tinner and coppersmith. He came to Galveston in 1838, starting in the hardware business with W.R. Wilson in a small wooden building where the first issues of the *Galveston Daily News* were being printed. When Davie and Wilson severed business ties, Davie continued the business and built here one of the first brick buildings in the city. It was where Gail Borden's Condensed Milk was first sold. Unfortunately, this first building was lost when it was razed to make room for the neighboring Continental Hotel. Next to the hotel, on the east, is the present-day four-story building that housed the J.P. Davie Hardware Company. It sat largely vacant between 1973 and 1986, when George and Cynthia Mitchell undertook its restoration following damage from Hurricane Alicia and a 1983 fire.

Galveston News Building
2108 Mechanic Street

When the first edition of the *Daily News* rolled off the press on April 11, 1842, its founders likely had no idea that theirs would become the oldest continuously published newspaper in Texas. It was published originally by George French, and the original offices were based out of a single-story building on Tremont Street. During the Civil War, the paper was briefly published in Houston, but following the war, it returned to the island, this time occupying three floors of an iron-fronted building on Market Street. In 1884, the paper moved into a new brick building designed by Nicholas Clayton.

Designed in the Neo-Renaissance style, Clayton's Galveston News Building was constructed in 1884. It hosted the offices and production plant of the *Galveston Daily News*, the most influential daily paper published in the state during the 1870s and the 1880s. At the time it was built, it was the first structure designed to be expressly used for the production of a newspaper. At the same time, in October 1885, the publishers also founded the *Dallas Morning News* as a satellite newspaper. During the 1960s, Clayton's design was covered with plaster panels, which were not removed until the mid-1990s. During this period, in 1965, the paper moved to its 8522 Teichman Road facility, where it remains today. Renamed the *Galveston County Daily News* on November 1, 1993, the paper branched out off the island and began covering all of the county.

Galveston Cotton Exchange and Board of Trade Building
2102 Mechanic Street

The Galveston Cotton Exchange was the first textile-trading building established in the state. The original structure, when completed in 1878, was touted as one of the most magnificent buildings in Texas. Prior to the Civil War, there was no need for an organized association of cotton buyers and sellers, as merchants would purchase cotton directly from growers at an agreed-on price and then would sell it for a profit. However, following the war, the production of cotton increased and the railroad industry expanded, resulting in the interests of cotton buyers and sellers no longer being aligned, which led to court battles and, eventually, Galveston cotton merchants forming their own association, as did the growers, called the Galveston Cotton Exchange.

The exchange's building, completed in December 1878, held a vast hall that measured eighty-three by sixty-three feet and sported a floor inlaid with walnut and oak, as was the interior work. The opening of the building, with its elite party, made the national news. In the late 1930s, it was decided that a more modern and air-conditioned building was needed to house the organization. That original building was razed and replaced with a Ben

Architect Ben Milam designed this more modern building for the Galveston Cotton Exchange to replace an 1879 Cotton Exchange building already on-site. It was the first Texas cotton brokerage and only the third cotton exchange in the United States when it was created in 1873. It closed in 1967 and today is missing its entryway's polished granite framing. *Author's collection.*

Milam–designed Art Deco–style structure completed in 1941 and located on the same site. By the mid-twentieth century, however, the cotton industry had begun to decline drastically, and railroad transportation was challenged as well, eventually leading to the end of the Galveston Cotton Exchange in 1967. Most recently, the building was used as office space; it has since been converted into residential space.

C.F. Marschner Building
1916 Mechanic Street

Looking at this building, you can clearly see its former use as C.F. Marschner's headquarters for the Texas Bottling Works, by the sign above the door. However, it also served as the residence of C.F. and Marie Marschner's family. It was erected in 1905–6 by local contractor Otto Haase. Shortly before its completion, C.F. died, leaving his widow the business to operate with the assistance of their sons. It was the first company in Galveston to

The C.F. Marschner Building housed both the Texas Bottling Works and the family residence of C.F. and Marie Marschner. When C.F. died, his widow took over operation of the business with her sons. It was the first company to bottle distilled water. *Author's collection.*

bottle distilled water. Texas Bottling Works remained until 1929, when Triple XXX Bottling moved in, with Otto Marschner as its general manager in the 1930s. Triple XXX Bottling continued to operate here until the mid-1940s, then the plant turned to bottling soft drinks until the 1960s, became storage space and, later, housed classic automobiles.

Sydnor Auction House
2200 Strand Street

While not the only location for slave sales and auctions in Galveston, John Seabrook Sydnor's Auction House, located across the street from General Granger's headquarters, was the most prominent. While slave auctions were more common in the Deep South, Sydnor's in Galveston, as well as at least one in Houston, were heavily attended. Sydnor was a leading figure in antebellum Galveston: he was a sergeant on the city board of alderman

Auctions for the sale of enslaved people were common among virtually every community that participated in chattel slavery. This was one location along the Strand where such auctions would take place. Commercial buildings have been located here since the early days of Galveston. The current building was constructed following the 1900 Storm, as the Moody's atrium landed on the 1896 building during the hurricane, crushing it. The current building dates to after the 1900 Storm, as the Moody's atrium landed on the 1896 building, crushing it. *Author's collection.*

and mayor of Galveston, served in the coast guard, helped establish schools, organized the police and fire departments and developed a city market, chamber of commerce and railroads. He was prominent in the cotton industry and, in 1845, built a brick wharf where he constructed a storage warehouse. Through the 1850s, Sydnor also was a leading slave dealer on the island, holding public auctions at this establishment. He moved to New York and went into a brokerage business when his interests following the Civil War in Galveston began to evaporate.

Absolute Equality Mural/Site of the Osterman Building
Twenty-Second and Strand Streets

Painted on the eastern wall of Old Galveston Square is the Absolute Equality mural, designed by commissioned artist Reginald C. Adams and his team of artists, the Creatives. The mural reimagines an approach to monuments and memorials to highlight the nation's diversity. The five-thousand-square-foot art installation displays five portals, each telling a new thread of the story: enslaved Africans being marched onto ships; Harriet Tubman; Abraham Lincoln holding the Emancipation Proclamation; General Granger, flanked by an African American Union soldier, issuing General Order No. 3 on Juneteenth; and a parade of people marching in pursuit of Absolute Equality, incorporating that phrase into the mural's graphics. The mural overlooks the site of the Osterman Building, which served as General Granger's headquarters in 1865. A plaque sits just beyond the mural, near the parking lot and sidewalk, that commemorates Juneteenth on the site where Granger likely issued the orders. The Juneteenth Legacy Project plans to sustain the art installation in perpetuity.

Boone Powell Mardi Gras Arch
Mechanic and Twenty-Fourth Streets

This arch is the only one remaining of seven previously standing colorful structures built throughout downtown Galveston to usher in the return of Mardi Gras in 1986 by island oilman, businessman and historical preservationist George P. Mitchell in 1985. It emerged from an idea by Galveston's Dancie Perugini Ware in the mid-1980s, who came across a photograph showing four colorful festival arches for Saengerfest in 1881.

The Boone Powell Mardi Gras Arch was built for a Mardi Gras celebration in 1986 and as a Texas sesquicentennial salute. This arch near the Tremont Hotel was one of several, in various styles, built throughout the history of the celebration. The Powell arch was one of seven that year and evokes the feeling of the sailing ships that called Galveston home. *Author's collection.*

This led to a more modern take on the designs. An eighth arch was added the following year, all of them intended to be temporary. However, the Tremont House arch remained due to its popularity. Several architects had been built commissioned to design and build the arches; this one was by Boone Powell. In 2002, the arch underwent an extensive restoration. This colorful structure is made of up pennants, rigging, and masts, evoking a nautical theme.

MARKET AND POSTOFFICE STREETS

U.S. National Bank Building
2201 Market Street

The iconic United States National Bank Building sits with its front entry, with clock above, angled at the intersection of Kempner/Avenue D and Market Streets. When it was founded in 1874, it became the last of the thirty-three banks chartered in this country that used the now-forbidden "United States" in their name. Originally, when the Kempner family founded the bank, it was named Island City Savings Bank. They changed it to Texas Bank & Trust Company in 1902 and, finally, to the aforementioned—and last— name on December 21, 1923. In 1926, the federal government banned the usage of the words *reserve*, *federal* or *United States* in bank names. Those that already had them incorporated were grandfathered in.

Cullen/Frost Bankers eventually took ownership of all capital stock in this bank and the Sugar Land State Bank. The previous bank would continue to operate separately from Frost for nearly two decades. When Cullen/Frost folded U.S. National Bank into Frost in 2000, the last bank using the federally forbidden "United States National Bank" title ceased to exist.

City National Bank Building
2219 Market Street

City National Bank opened on Market Street in 1920. This grand dame of banks gave clients the impressive visage of an institution that could manage the security of their money. It was Neoclassical in design, and its ornate plasterwork, Greek motifs inside and out, tall marble wall panels and columns all marketed the bank building as reassuring, safe and important. Chicago architects Weary & Alford designed the bank for William L. Moody, who founded the bank in 1907 and moved the location here when it was completed.

While the name of the bank changed in 1953 to Moody National Bank, the building retains the carved "City National Bank" above its entrance. By the time the early 1960s rolled around, the bank's leadership had constructed a new, more modern bank a few blocks away, abandoning this historic building. In 1972, Mary Moody Northen donated the building to the county, which operated the Galveston County Historical Museum out of the space from 1978 until the fall of 2008, when Hurricane Ike struck the island. Ike filled the building's basement with water and destroyed its HVAC system, which left the building and its artifacts susceptible to decay.

Following Ike, the museum left the building, and Ross Moody gave it a go on restoration and rehabilitation of the building for residential and event space but ultimately donated the building and project to the Galveston Historical Foundation in 2020. It is one of twenty-two buildings that the historical foundation owns and contains two bedrooms suites for residential space, with the main floor being available for small parties or events.

City National Bank was founded in December 1907 by William Moody Jr. This building was completed in 1920 and would later serve as the Galveston County Historical Museum until 2008, when Hurricane Ike severely damaged the building. The assets were later moved to the county courthouse, and while the building has been unused since, it is undergoing extensive restorations. *Author's collection.*

E.S. Levy Building
2221–2225 Market Street

Also known as the National Hotel Building, the E.S. Levy Building was built in 1896 by architect Charles W. Bulger. Originally, this space housed the Tremont Opera house and, before that, a newspaper office until an 1869 fire. When it was redesigned to serve as home for the E.S. Levy department store in 1896, Bulger retained some of the walls for the structure and added a fifth story in 1899. The E.S. Levy & Company clothing store operated for more than a century in Galveston.

Abraham Levy and his business partner opened a small storefront along the 2200 block of Market Street in 1877. The new firm of Levy & Weiss sold clothing and furnishings for men and boys. When Abraham died in 1879, his son Edward S. Levy assumed control of the business, changing it to E.S. Levy & Company. When they opened this new storefront, the upscale clothing store operated on the ground floor while eighty professional suites occupied the upper floors. At the time of the 1900 Storm, the United States Weather Bureau's Texas offices were located here, headed by Isaac Cline.

Levy's outgrew this location within a few years and, in 1917, moved one block to the north to a location with more room on Postoffice Street, which would continue to expand throughout the 1960s. Levy's maintained its focus on men and boys until the 1930s, when it expanded to include offerings for women and girls. Despite its growth and growing diversity of offerings, the decline of Galveston's downtown along with the advent of shopping malls led Levy's to close in 1979, severing operations after 102 years. In 2001, the building was redeveloped to serve as a mixed-use space. It is also known as the National Hotel Artist Lofts and includes an art exhibit space known as the Proletariat Gallery, established in 2015.

Fire Station No. 3
2828 Market Street

When Star State Company No. 3 was formed in 1859, it became the third firehouse on the island. The city constructed the company its own firehouse in 1860. It stood for forty years before being leveled during the 1900 hurricane. The firehouse standing now replaced the original one on the same footprint. It is the only one remaining from the Victorian period

The Star State Company No. 3 Engine House was rebuilt in 1903, following its destruction during the 1900 Storm, a short distance from downtown. It operated as a fire station until it was decommissioned in the 1960s. It was the first station in the city to be integrated, in 1959. It is the only remaining firehouse from the Victorian period on the island. *Author's collection.*

on the island. Originally, the building sported a parapet and balcony at the center of its façade, but the 1915 hurricane damaged the building, removing some of the early architectural elements.

The addition of a concrete face placed on the building around 1950s further detracted from its historical appearance. Later that decade, in 1957, Star State Company No. 3 became the first firehouse in Galveston to integrate with African American firefighters. The building was continued in use until its decommissioning during the 1960s. Later, the city's water department operated out of the building before finally vacating it for city storage. The Galveston Historical Foundation acquired the building in 2017 and is currently reconstructing and preserving the historical integrity of the building.

Garbade, Eiband & Company Building
2205 Postoffice Street

This building houses the oldest operating business in its original location downtown. Not only is the structure historic, but the businesses inside were also landmarks all their own. The department store of Garbade, Eiband & Company was formed by Henry Eiband, Henry Garbade and Thomas McCrea. They hung their shingle in September 1895 in a small building located at this site. In 1914, the partners acquired all the buildings on three lots. Following the purchase, they consolidated and remodeled them, adding a fourth floor in the process.

The original core of the building dates to 1870, before the great fire. The middle portion of the row was originally the Ballinger & Jack Building, owned by one of Galveston's most prominent law firms at the time. From 1875 until 1890, the Supreme Court of Texas actually sat in this building, later becoming part of Eiband's in 1900. The partners split the business in 1922, Garbade taking the building and Eiband becoming the owner of the business operations. In 1965, the building underwent rehabilitation, involving remodeling the first and third floors, modernizing the exterior and adding dozens of new lines of merchandise. A more historic rehabilitation came in 1995.

The Pix Building
2128 Postoffice Street

The three-story Pix Building, located catty-corner from Eiband's, was built in 1858. Constructed of brick in the Greek Revival style, this was one of a handful of buildings owned by Charles Hodgeson Pix in Galveston. Pix had come to Galveston with his family from England in 1838. He was one of the early English merchants on the island and imported his goods directly from London. Starting a business as Pix and Burney, ship brokers, he opened his first location at No. 6 Strand in 1839. In short order, he owned the entire half block on the north side of Postoffice between Twenty-First and Twenty-Second Streets, including this building.

The Pix is one of the oldest buildings downtown. It was partly rebuilt in 1875, and in both 1909 and 1954, the first floor was remodeled, while the front wall was rebuilt in 1948 with new brick. Having been constructed prior to the Civil War, it saw action during the conflict. The signal corps of the Confederate army occupied the building in 1864 following the Battle of Galveston. The Merchants Club occupied the third floor for its meetings in 1866. Then, from 1906 to 1924, the *Galveston Tribune* was printed here before it moved operations to the Leon and H. Blum Building on Mechanic. In recent years, it has housed Michael's Jewelry (from 1938 until the 1980s) and retail and a coffee shop.

Galveston Opera House
2012–2020 Postoffice Street

Postoffice Street got itself a nice little boost in 1894–95. New Orleans–based theatrical impresario Henry Greenwall decided to leave the twenty-three-year-old Tremont Opera House (located where the Levy Building is today) in 1894. Instead, he persuaded a group of Galveston businessmen to invest in a new theater. They would construct a 1,500-seat theater combined with a fifty-six-room hotel. Designed by Frank Cox, a little-known New Orleans architect, in the Richardsonian Romanesque style, the opera house sports red pressed brick, terra-cotta ornamentation across the front façade and a huge arched entryway.

The Grand 1894 Opera House, seen here next to O'Malley's Pub, opened in 1895. Since that time, this downtown stalwart has survived the 1900 Storm, the 1915 hurricane and Hurricanes Carla and Ike. It began as a live performing arts venue, passed through the vaudeville era and then served as a movie house until 1974; it has since returned to live performances. *Author's collection.*

When the opera house opened, it started first as a venue for live performances such as plays, operas, vaudeville performances and more. When film became more prevalent and popular, it served as a movie house until 1974. Along the way, the interior would get altered here and there—changes that were suitable for the way the space was being used. Unfortunately, these changes were historically inappropriate, and the building eventually suffered from insufficient maintenance. When the theater closed in 1974, the new Galveston County Cultural Arts Council purchased the building with the goal to rehabilitate the building back to its era of prowess. Throughout the 1980s, the opera house received restoration to its stage, auditorium, lobby and exterior. It stands as the only one of Henry Greenwall's theaters that remain. It continues to host live performances year-round.

U.S. Custom House, Post Office and Courtroom
1927 Postoffice Street

Known as the Old Customhouse, the Galveston Custom House is a two-story Greek Revival brick building that was constructed between 1858 and 1861. Designed by the United States Treasury architect Ammi B. Young in 1854, it is thought to be the first Galveston building designed by a proper architect. The design ended up being slightly altered by contractors Charles Blaney Cluskey and Edwin Ward Moore. Inside, the building houses the customhouse as well as a post office and the United States district court.

Much of the building was prefabricated in the North and shipped to the site, including the cast-iron columns, cornices and other wrought-iron features. Construction of the building was halted briefly by a yellow fever epidemic in 1858 that interrupted construction until just prior to the Civil War. Even then, the building was used only briefly before war broke out and it was turned over to the Confederate forces. During the Battle of Galveston, in 1863, the building took shelling and also was the site of the Bread Riot, initiated by the wives of absent Confederate soldiers when they stormed the building demanding flour. The war officially ended for Galveston on June 2, 1865, when Union forces took possession of the site by raising the American flag. In 1891, a new customhouse was built, relegating this building to housing offices; it continued to house the post office. A restoration of the building took place in 1967, and three years later, it was listed on the National Register of Historic Places. Despite a damaging boiler explosion in 1978, the Old Customhouse was repaired and stands strong to this day.

Central Drug Store
2116 Postoffice Street

Today housing the Witchery, a shop for those with a mystical bent, the old Central Drug Store's original purpose is easily revered here by its owners. Among the shelves filled with books on the occult, candles, books, tarot cards and more are old apothecary bottles, the original tile and many original fixtures and cabinetry. While there are so many historic buildings in Galveston, there are only a handful downtown where the original purpose of the operation is immediately evident.

Site of Turf Athletic Club/Western Room/Studio Lounge
2214 Market Street

There are so many historic buildings still standing in Galveston that sometimes the ones that *are* gone need some attention. Located here once was the Turf Athletic Club, the headquarters of the Maceo syndicate, a three-story building that housed a casino, two restaurants and the athletic club. A bookmaking parlor was located on the ground floor, and there, bettors could wager on any sporting event in the country, with horse races being broadcast live on the PA system. A raid by the Texas Rangers in 1935 didn't deter the Maceos either. Instead, the Maceos revamped the building, enhancing its legitimate façade. On the first floor, at the front of the building, the Maceos added the Turf Grill, while the second floor opened up to become the Studio Lounge; the Maceo offices were on the third floor.

On March 8, 1948, fire swallowed the top floor of the club. The Maceos came back, thriving instead on the second floor, and the building reopened. Eventually, law enforcement clamped down on vice in Galveston, and Sam Maceo died in 1951, followed by Rose in 1954, thus ending the Free State of Galveston (and, some say, nearly ending Galveston). In 1968, 2216 Market Street, along with the rest of the block, was demolished.

THE REST OF DOWNTOWN

Santa Fe Building
123 Rosenberg Avenue

Constructed as the Santa Fe Building, and today known as Shearn Moody Plaza, Galveston's historic train station houses the Galveston Railroad Museum. Galveston's railroad passenger terminal was constructed in 1913. It underwent a massive expansion and remodeling project designed by Santa Fe's Chicago-based corporate architect E.A Harrison in 1932, providing spectacular Art Deco detailing and pulling together the building's disparate parts. Its white glazed brick and terra-cotta stands in stark contrast to so many of the Strand's ruddy nineteenth-century buildings.

The south half of the building is the 1913 portion and was constructed to serve as a central passenger station for Galveston's railway system and to house the general offices of the Atchison, Topeka & Santa Fe Railroad's Gulf lines, called the Gulf, Colorado and Santa Fe Railway (GC&SF). The expanded 1932 portion includes an eleven-story tower and an eight-story north wing. Standing on the Strand, looking toward the Santa Fe Building, one notices that it is slightly off its axis. The central register and north wing are additions to the south wing, which began its life as an addition to the preceding passenger terminal building of 1897. In 1964, the Galveston office of the Santa Fe Railroad closed, with the company's last passenger train stopping here three years later. The Moody Foundation bought the then-empty passenger station and office building in 1976. Following a restoration, it opened in 1982 as home to the Galveston Railroad Museum. It became a Recorded Texas Historic Landmark in 1983.

Old Quarter Acoustic Café
413 Twentieth Street

The Old Quarter bar opened first in downtown Houston, near the corner of Congress and Austin Streets, in 1965. Founders Rex "Wrecks" Bell and Cecil Slayton opened it to replace a previous bar, the Yellow Cab Club. When Slayton left, Dale Soffar partnered with Bell, but Bell left for Nashville in the 1970s, leaving Dale Soffar as the sole owner of the operation. It became best known as the venue for the live album by Townes Van Zandt *Live at the Old Quarter, Houston, Texas*, recorded in 1973 and released in 1977. He closed the location in 1979 but returned to Texas and reopened the café in Galveston in 1996 before retiring in 2016. This new iteration is small, essentially no more than a drafty room in a 1914 three-story building, located next to the Grand 1894 Opera House. Despite its small stature, familiar draws such as Ray Wylie Hubbard, Hayes Carll (who also tended bar here for three years) and Ramblin' Jack Elliott have transformed the café into a hub for Galveston's own music scene.

Pier 21 and the Middle Passage
2100 Harborside Drive

Pier 21 has evolved into Galveston's waterfront entertainment and dining district. Located on Galveston's harbor in the Strand area, Pier 21 features a variety of attractions. Visit the Texas Seaport Museum, which houses the 1877 tall ship *Elissa*; dine at a variety of restaurants; see docked cruise ships before they depart; catch a glimpse of dolphins (and maybe a manatee); stay at the Harbor House Hotel and Marina. The pier has one of the best views of this side of the harbor.

Located at the Texas Seaport Museum is a historical marker commemorating the Middle Passage. Galveston was one of forty-eight known ports of entry in the United States for enslaved Africans during the transatlantic slave trade. Millions of captive Africans perished during the transatlantic crossing. The marker shows the routes taken during the eighteenth and nineteenth centuries.

Texas Seaport Museum
2200 Harborside Drive

The Texas Seaport Museum is the home of the famed 1877 tall ship *Elissa*, designated as one of America's Treasures by the National Trust for Historic Preservation. You can walk the decks of the barque and imagine scenes of days gone by on the open seas. In the adjacent museum and theater, you can witness the story of the *Elissa*'s rescue from the scrapyard and the restoration that brought her back to her glory days and made her seaworthy once again. Additionally, at the museum, learn more about how Galveston served as one of America's most important immigration ports.

The Galveston Historic Seaport is home to the 1877 tall ship *Elissa* and so much more. In addition to the square-rigged iron barque (one of only three active barques in the world), adjacent to the ship is the Texas Seaport Museum, where you can learn more about the Galveston port, the harbor and Galveston's role in 1880s immigration. *Author's collection.*

Ocean Star Offshore Drilling Rig and Museum
2202 Wharf Road

The Ocean Star is a retired jack-up drilling rig that once operated in the Gulf of Mexico from 1969 to 1984. There, it drilled over two hundred wells. In 1995, the Offshore Energy Center (OEC) purchased the Ocean Star, refurbishing it and opening it as a museum in 1997. It is located just one block off the Strand and a short walk down from the Texas Seaport Museum. Self-guided, the rig houses a museum and education facility that investigates geological exploration such as drilling, oil and gas production and offshore drilling equipment.

Battleship Texas
Pier 21

On August 31, 2022, Battleship Texas made her way from her long-standing home near the San Jacinto Monument in LaPorte to Galveston. For years, the battleship, famed for its service in World War I and World War II, suffered from sitting in the brackish water, with limited resources to counteract its effects, while remaining open to the public. Unfortunately, time caught up with the battleship and she closed to the public, eventually being transported to Galveston. While dry-docked in Galveston Harbor, the vessel will be displayed. While opportunities are no longer available for viewing during the restoration of the ship, as of this writing, the project is nearing its end, meaning that the ship should once again be open to the public, rather than only being able to be seen from the docks or from a harbor boat. There is a strong likelihood that the new permanent home of Battleship Texas will remain Galveston for the near future.

Mallory Line Warehouse/Cruise Terminal
Pier 23–26

The Mallory Line Warehouse, now a Galveston Cruise Terminal, sits at Pier 23–26. The Mallory Line, operated by the New York & Texas Steamship Co. out of New York from 1866 to 1932, was one of the oldest family-owned passenger lines in the coastwide trade. The line connected New York City with Galveston, later expanding its route offerings to New Orleans,

Cruise ships are a common site in Galveston, and they keep getting bigger. In 1974, the port hosted its first cruise ship. By the 1990s, it was aggressively seeking out modern cruise ships to port at Galveston. When the ship *Celebration* from Carnival Cruise Lines began docking here in 2000, it broke the longtime trend of older and smaller cruise ships docking in the port. *Author's collection.*

Louisiana; Mobile, Alabama; and Havana, Cuba. Later it was purchased by the Consolidated Steamship Lines and then by the Atlantic, Gulf and West Indies SS Co., which continued to provide service under the Mallory name and flag until 1932, when it combined the Mallory routes with those of the old Clyde Line under the new name Clyde-Mallory Line. This was sold in 1949 to the Bull Line, and the Mallory company name disappeared. In 2000, the Texas Cruise Ship Terminal on Galveston Island was rededicated during ceremonies that September. Here the Galveston Cruise Terminal marked a $10.6 million renovation and refurbishment of the Mallory Line Warehouse at Pier 25. It served as the single greatest investment in improvements in the port's 175-year history. Three days later, Carnival Cruise Lines' vessel MS *Celebration* made its inaugural voyage from the island.

Marine Building
305 Twenty-First Street

German immigrant Samson Heindenheimer built the Heidenheimer Brothers Marine Building in 1876. Heidenheimer was already in business prior to the Civil War, working as a street vendor. The Civil War proved to be prosperous for Heindenheimer, as he built up his business by dealing in cotton and blockade running. Then, with his brothers, he opened a wholesale grocery business, which operated under a variety of names at this location until 1904.

A division of the Morgan Steamship Line, the Suderman & Dolson Stevedores, moved into the building in 1904, forever altering the moniker of the building. Since then, it has changed hands several times. Considered a commercial and historic landmark, the Marine Building underwent restoration in 1984–85.

Star Drug Store Co. Building
510 Tremont Street

Prominent real estate family the Scanlons purchased land in downtown Galveston. They built the Levy Building and the Star Drug Store, hiring Nicholas Clayton to design their new buildings. Clayton attached façades sporting asymmetrical window groupings. The original Star Drug Store was wood. When Charles J. Michaelis, local druggist, bought the building

Galveston's historic Star Drug Store touts itself as the oldest drugstore in Texas. It was built in 1886 and then, in 1906, purchased by local druggist Charles Michaelis, who converted the wood structure to brick. It became operational in 1917, became the first desegregated lunch counter in Galveston and changed hands several times, continuing to maintain history. A fire closed the store in 1998, but it was renovated and reopened in 2001. *Author's collection.*

in 1906, he hired a contractor who converted the building to brick with zero compromise to Clayton's design in a $15,000 project that was completed in 1909. By 1917, the Star Drug Store was in operation, hosting a horseshoe-shaped tile soda fountain counter.

George Clampitt and Grady Dickinson purchased the store in the 1920s, operating it until 1982. Together they maintained the integrity of the drugstore. They also became a part of history when the Star became Galveston's first desegregated lunch counter. Several times, ownership changed over the years, but the building closed indefinitely following a massive fire on Friday, March 13, 1998. In November 2001, the Tilts family purchased and restored the building, including the façade, two loft apartments upstairs, the neon Coca-Cola sign outside and the drugstore. In 2008, Hurricane Ike filled the store with more than six and a half feet of water. It managed to reopen in three months.

Martini Theater
524 Twenty-First Street

The Martini Theatre was built for Attilio Martini in 1937. Martini had originally opened his theater in the Grand Opera House in 1924, moving to this location when construction was finished. At one time, the Martini family owned eight theaters on the island. However, as television caught on, the popularity of theaters began to diminish. This theater, seating 990 and designed in the Art Deco style, was remodeled in 1969 but eventually closed in 1975. Like many of its contemporaries, it was originally used for both vaudeville and motion pictures. During the 1940s, while it was one of several downtown theaters, it was considered the most up-to-date.

The Martini remains one of Galveston's few examples of Art Deco architecture. The stuccoed masonry theater, with its marquee on the southwest corner, has a recessed tiled entrance with a box office, and the rest of the front connects to other commercial buildings. The original tall neon marquee was lost numerous years ago, while the large orange letters spelling out the theater's name remain. The building has suffered from storms that have damaged the interior and exterior. In 2013, the Martini Theater was put on the Galveston Historical Foundation's Heritage at Risk List.

First Presbyterian Church
1903 Church Street

Not long after the founding of Galveston, the island became a bustling metropolis of some three hundred people. Until that time, Roman Catholicism was really the only religion being practiced, and the preaching of Protestantism was prohibited. However, in 1836, the first Protestant sermon was given in Galveston out in the open near the old Navy Yard, located on the flats at the foot of Twenty-Fourth Street. A few years later, another sermon was given; this led to the formal organization, in 1840, of the Presbyterian congregation. With the assistance of missionaries from the United States, the congregation met from 1843 to 1872 in a wooden church building, the first church building on the island.

When the congregation organized, its original building was known as the Academy, located on the northwest corner of this intersection. It was finished in 1943. Construction of the current iteration, a Romanesque building, began in 1872, taking until 1889 to complete. The church managed to escape harm during the Great Fire of 1885, housing in its classes students from schools that had not been so lucky. It is considered one of the best examples of Norman architecture in the region. Designed by Nicholas Clayton, it managed to withstand various hurricanes and tropical storms until it was heavily damaged in 1961 by Hurricane Carla. It was restored in 1962 and designated a Recorded Texas Historic Landmark in 1968.

St. Mary's Cathedral
2011 Church Street

Reverend John Odin was appointed to be the resident vice-prefect of Texas in 1840. He traveled to Galveston from New Orleans in early 1841 and found a small community of Catholics ready to build a church for their congregation. Over the next few months, Odin raised funds with the help of Colonel Michael B. Menard and Dr. Nicholas Labadie. In February 1842, Odin dedicated the completed small rectangular building, adding to the property later a small sacristy, thirty benches for the parishioners and a five-room cottage as the episcopal residence.

In 1845, Odin, now a bishop, purchased five hundred thousand bricks from Belgium, planning to use them in the construction of a larger, permanent church. Parishioners moved the small frame church out into the street and began to construct their new church right on the spot in 1847. On November 26, 1848, the cathedral was dedicated. Following a major flood in 1875, the tower was crowned with a statue of Mary, Star of the Sea, which has withstood all storms since; it is one of the few buildings in Galveston that survived the 1900 Storm with only minimal damage.

Saint Mary's Cathedral stands as Galveston's oldest surviving church. Preserved in its original Gothic cathedral style, it features fine stained-glass windows and impressive altars. It is the primary cathedral of the Archdiocese of Galveston-Houston and is the mother church of the Catholic church in Texas, as well as a minor basilica. It was named a Texas state historic landmark in 1968 and has been listed on the National Register of Historic Places since 1973.

Scottish Rite Cathedral
2128 Church Street

Back in 2007, visitors on the Galveston Historic Homes Tour got a rare chance to view the inside of Galveston's Scottish Rite Cathedral, a place only Masons and their families had a chance to peer into. One thing was evident: the building has been maintained over the years, never restored. Prior to this building, the site housed another Masonic cathedral, which was destroyed by fire, but its Italian marble stairway and wainscoting were salvaged and installed in the new building.

Built in 1929 in the Art Deco style by Texas architect Alfred C. Finn, the building is a time capsule that has barely been touched. Upstairs is a majestic theater, with hand-painted canvas backdrops and a 1,256-pipe organ, which has not changed—except new upholstery for the seats during the 1960s. A high-ceilinged space with an elevated orchestra pit, known as "the ballroom," also remains, with its original cream-and-blue color scheme from 1929. Also, inside is a library with records dating to when Texas was a republic, the old recreation room with its original pool table and a ground-floor lodge room that sports an Egyptian theme: cartouches, vultures, an ankh and lotus flowers. It is now used for special events.

1937 U.S. Custom House, Post Office and Courthouse
601 Rosenberg Street

Also known as the Galveston Federal Building, the U.S. Post Office and Courthouse serves as the federal court for the Galveston Division of the United States District Court for the Southern District of Texas. Designed in the Art Deco style by architect Alfred C. Finn and constructed in 1937, it has represented the federal government for more than six decades.

The structure, standing at seven stories, is clad with porous fossiliferous limestone, utilizing a common practice in the 1930s of using regional materials whenever possible. Originally it was planned to be faced with brick, but local congressman Joseph J. Mansfield and Fred Papst, the collector of customs, urged the Treasury Department to use limestone, feeling it was a better fit for a federal building. The construction took place during a period of unprecedented federal construction throughout the United States during this time.

The Galveston Federal Building, also known as the U.S. Post Office and Courthouse, serves as the federal court for the Galveston Division of the U.S. District Court for the Southern District of Texas. Designed in the Art Deco style, it has represented the federal government in Galveston for sixty years. Get as close as you can to the exterior limestone cladding and see innumerable marine shell fossils. *Author's collection.*

An earlier Romanesque building was constructed in the early 1890s on this very spot to replace the previous customshouse and courthouse built in the 1850s. Galveston grew so fast that the federal government needed a larger building, then another, then finally this one. Originally the post office was located on the first floor, the postal inspectors on the second, various government offices on the third, the Customs Department on the fourth, then petit and grand jury space on the fifth floor. Judges, U.S. attorneys, U.S. marshals and the ceremonial courtroom were all located on the sixth floor, while the seventh floor housed the Bureaus of Navigation and Agriculture. Though the tenants have changed somewhat, the basic function of the buildings remains as it was when it was constructed.

Galveston Book Store/Bienville Social Club
323 Tremont Street

The stretch of buildings here, housing the private Bienville Social and its neighbor, the Galveston Bookstore, dates to the 1880s. The bookstore is the most complete new and used bookstore on the island. It features a great

Its facade fronted with a mural of books, the Galveston Book Shop has been a fixture of downtown Galveston since 1991. Two stories of new, used and vintage books, along with racks of comics and vinyl, climb the shelves, with a particularly great section on local and state history—all located in a historic building. *Author's collection.*

section on local and regional history that is unmatched in even the largest bookstores in Houston.

The Bienville Social portion of the buildings was restored following Hurricane Ike. The goal was a venue with a New Orleans feel while retaining the unique Galveston architecture, including an original skylight and the masonry. The name pays homage to Jean-Baptiste Le Moyne de Bienville, one of New Orleans' original colonizers, who served as Louisiana governor from 1701 to 1743. Bienville was responsible for the original plans of Vieux Carre, the French Quarter. The social club's courtyard is one of the few remaining downtown.

Model Laundry & Dye Works Building
513–525 Church

Take a look up and you can see the "Model Laundry and Dye Works" ghost sign peering through the ages of faded paint and grime at you. Of the three sides of this two-story building that are visible, this is the only one that remains red brick. The building represents a later type of commercial architecture one does not find readily in Galveston. William A. Johnson, well-known nationally in the laundry business, constructed the building. He had arrived in Galveston in 1909 to take over Model Laundry and Dye Works, a business in operation since 1888 that had since deteriorated. According to Sanborn Maps, the building was constructed in 1913; improvements followed in 1914 and 1915. A laundry business at the time was considered extremely progressive for the period, and this one served as the island's only steam laundry. The building continued to be used for laundry-related purposes through 1970.

First Lutheran Church and the Lyceum
2401 Winnie Avenue

The Galveston Lyceum Society was chartered in 1845, during the Republic of Texas period. Shortly after its founding, the society built the lyceum building as part of an education movement that constructed specialized meeting halls in communities. These societies established educational gatherings, events and forums, bringing together the community at its cultural centers, which often also housed libraries.

This lyceum was the second formed in the republic; the first was established in Austin in 1839. Held specifically in this building were a variety of lectures and concerts as well as debates that centered on annexation, slavery, temperance and Native Americans. Known simply as Lyceum Hall, this building hosted the First Lutheran Church's first Sunday service in 1852, on Easter. The church would go on to rent the Lyceum for seventy-five dollars annually. After a year, the church purchased two adjacent lots from a German organization, which also maintained a German school. A few years later, the church bought the Lyceum building and moved it from the corner of Winnie and Twenty-Fifth Street to the corner of Winnie and Twenty-Fourth. During the week, the building was occupied as a school, and on Sunday, it was transformed into an auditorium.

The Lyceum is in downtown Galveston. Built in the 1840s, it served as a philosophical meeting center and entertainment venue for the community. The First Lutheran Church purchased the building in 1854, turning it into a worship center for the church and the first public school in Galveston. It is an event venue presently. *Author's collection.*

With a swelling congregation, the church voted to construct a new wood-frame church for its services. It was dedicated in 1868, and the lyceum building remained, becoming home to Sunday school and social gatherings. It quickly became one of the largest Lutheran churches in the state. In 1915, the church underwent a transformation, being given a brick veneer. Additionally, the lyceum was attached to the west wing as an annex for church overflow and Sunday school. During the remodeling project, the original slab from the Galveston Lyceum Society was found and can be seen inside the narthex of the sanctuary built in 1959. Today, the lyceum is a location used for weddings, meetings and social events.

Rosenberg Library
823 Tremont Street

The Rosenberg Library is the oldest continuously operating library in Texas, established in 1900. The library building was constructed a few years later, in 1902, in the Second Renaissance Revival style. Then, in 1905, it absorbed the collection of the recently defunct public library, which had been established as the Galveston Free Library, also known as the Galveston Mercantile Library, in 1871.

Named for its benefactor, Henry Rosenberg, the Rosenberg Library Association hired Alfred F. Rosenheim out of St. Louis to serve as its consulting architect for a design competition. Ultimately, the award went to Eames & Young for a design that was fireproof and featured two stories, a basement and a lecture hall. The library officially opened for inspection on June 22, 1904—Henry Rosenberg's birthday—and then to the public the following day. The Moody Memorial Wing, which opened in 1971, more than doubled the library's floor space and allowed for a children's library, a history center and several galleries to showcase its collections.

The building was inundated with floodwaters in 2008 during Hurricane Ike but suffered no structural damage. It has since undergone various renovations. Today the library is not only home to the public library but also served as headquarters of both the Galveston County library system and the Galveston and Texas History Center, which collects materials relating to Galveston and early Texas. The center's map collection, which includes maps and charts of the upper Gulf Coast, is nearly unrivaled.

Congregation B'nai Israel Temple
816 Twenty-Second Street

Organized by German Jewish immigrants in 1868, Congregation B'nai Israel is the oldest Jewish Reform congregation and the second chartered one in the state (right behind Houston's). Jews were among the numerous German immigrants who came to Texas during the 1840s. In Galveston, they established the first Jewish cemetery in the state (1852), held the first organized Jewish services in the state (1856) and organized the congregation on the island in 1868 and its chartering two years later.

By 1870, Congregation B'nai Israel was ready to build its sanctuary. The master of the Masonic Lodge of Texas, Philip C. Tucker Jr., laid the cornerstone. By the late 1880s, the congregation had grown enough that it needed a new synagogue. Texas architect Nicholas J. Clayton, famed for his religious structures, was commissioned to replace the old structure on its original site. His Victorian design, constructed in 1890, became an ornately detailed synagogue and landmark throughout the city.

As the congregation grew, members realized space was needed for their activities and decided to build the Henry Cohen Community House, named for its Rabbi Henry Cohen, in 1928. The community house was constructed on the lot next to the temple. The synagogue was used by the congregation until they sold it in the 1950s to the Masonic Lodge to use as their new Masonic Temple, moving to a newer synagogue once again. Their new synagogue is located just outside downtown and was designed by Holocaust survivor Tibor Beerman. The Masons simplified parts of the historical complex's façade, but the basic historical structure remains.

Trinity Episcopal Church
701 Twenty-Second Street

Trinity Episcopal Church is one of Galveston's oldest congregations, established on February 6, 1841, under the direction of Irish-born clergyman Reverend Benjamin Eaton. Their first church building, constructed in 1841 and completed the following June, was a simple frame church located on the southeastern corner of Twenty-Third and Winnie Streets. Unfortunately, it was brought down within a few months by a massive hurricane. The church reopened the following April once repairs were made. By the mid-1850s, the church was deemed too small for the congregation, and a larger church was planned at the opposite end of the block. Galveston architect John De Young was hired to design it, and the cornerstone of the Gothic-style brick church was laid on November 29, 1855. The church took two years to construct.

Ball High School
Twenty-First and Ball Avenue

A public school district, restricted then to "white or caucasian students" only, was organized in Galveston in 1881, authorized by a legislative act a few years earlier. In the summer of 1883, local dry goods businessman George Ball contributed $50,000 to the project. The end result consisted of twelve classrooms, two offices and an auditorium for grades eight through twelve. One early notable event came on October 12, 1894, when Ball High School's football team played the Agricultural and Mechanical College of Texas, now known as Texas A&M, in the college's first game. The Ball High Tornadoes lost 14–6.

When the 1900 Storm struck, the high school suffered extensive damage. Due to the death and destruction across the island, school attendance plummeted by nearly 25 percent, resulting in an excess of teachers. By the fall of 1901, classes had resumed here and student population increased dramatically by 1915. Two wings were added, creating six new classrooms, to accommodate the rapidly expanding student population, but it wasn't enough; overcrowding had become a problem again by 1924. At that point, those two wings were extended to accommodate additional classroom space. For the next thirty years, no more additions or improvements were made to the school, and it grew overpopulated and dilapidated. The high school moved to a new building in 1954 at Forty-First Street and Avenue O. The original building still stands, much altered, and houses the offices of the American Indemnity Company.

Reedy Chapel AME Church
2013 Broadway

Members of the African Methodist Episcopal Church congregation had been given land at Twentieth and Broadway by their White owners to establish a place of worship in 1848. They worshipped outside until a proper structure—the first of its kind in Texas—was built in 1866, the year following emancipation. The church building itself was constructed in 1863 and served as one of the locations of the public reading of General Order No. 3, announcing the emancipation of enslaved people, by General Granger on June 19, 1865. That church building was destroyed during the 1885 fire, but a new one quickly took its place. The Gothic Revival–style church building, constructed in 1886, was named for the congregation's second pastor, Reverend Houston Reedy. It managed to survive the 1900 Storm and was listed on the National Register of Historic Places in 1980.

Ashton Villa
2328 Broadway

This fully restored home, constructed in 1859, was one of the first brick structures in Texas built by slaves. Prominent hardware merchant and banker Colonel James Moreau Brown purchased four lots at the corner of Twenty-Fourth and Broadway on January 7, 1859, to build a home. Brown

In 1859, Colonel James Moreau Brown used and modified several architectural pattern books of the time to design his home, named Ashton Villa. Built using slave labor and European craftsmen, this was one of the first brick structures in the state. While the Emancipation Proclamation was read from numerous sites in Galveston, this is the most noteworthy. *Courtesy of the Texas State Archives.*

referenced multiple architectural pattern books and modified several plans to design the building, then utilized slave labor and European craftsmen to build this three-story brick house.

The home, built in the Victorian Italianate style, features ornate verandas stick out in contrast to its neighbors, topped by lintels made of cast iron. The walls of the home are thirteen inches thick, thus helping protect against humidity but also adding strength to the home to withstand the island's storms. Brown's wife, Rebecca Ashton, named the home Ashton Villa in honor of the Revolutionary War hero, and her ancestor, Lieutenant Isaac Ashton.

Just a few years after construction was finalized, the Civil War struck the island. Ashton Villa became the headquarters for the Confederate army, serving in that capacity throughout the war, save one period. During the fall of 1862, Galveston was surrendered to the Union, and Ashton Villa became their headquarters. The following January, however, Galveston was retaken, and the Confederates took back Ashton Villa during the Battle of

Known as the place where Union major general Gordon Granger announced the enforcement of the emancipation of enslaved peoples, Ashton Villa has a long history. During the Civil War, the two-year-old house became the headquarters of the Confederate army and served in that capacity throughout the war—except for a brief spell in the fall of 1862, when Galveston surrendered to the Union army, which also made the home its HQ. *Author's collection.*

Galveston. The home's greatest claim to fame, however, came at the end of the war. News of Abraham Lincoln's Emancipation Proclamation, issued on January 1, 1863, had yet to reach Texas and did not do so until after the Civil War had ended. On June 19, Union general Gordon Granger announced, throughout Galveston, that enslaved people were freed. While it has since been determined that General Granger gave his famous speech at his headquarters, the Ostermann Building, another speech location, one of several, was the balcony of Ashton Villa.

While Ashton Villa survived the 1900 Storm, the basement and lower floors were heavily damaged. The basement was filled in with sand during the island's rebuilding efforts following that storm, and the grounds were covered with two feet of soil. More than one hundred years later, it was severely damaged again, during Hurricane Ike. The El Mina Shrine Masonic order purchased the building and never made any appreciable alterations to the home. The order used the building as its offices and meeting hall until 1970, when it was put up for sale. Ashton Villa managed to avoid the wrecking ball with the help of the Galveston Historical Foundation. The foundation helped renovate the house, opening it four years later, and continues to operate the home to this day.

The Carriage House has been converted into an exhibit space that reflects the story of the emancipation story on the island. Open from Friday through Sundays, the exhibition "And Still We Rise…Galveston's Juneteenth Story" introduces the context and consequences of the 1865 announcement to the present day.

The Open Gates
2424 Broadway

Built for the Galveston merchant and banker George Sealy and his wife, Magnolia Willis Sealy, Open Gates was designed by the New York architectural firm of McKim, Mead & White. It is thought to be Stanford White's only design in the region. White designed it in the Neo-Renaissance style, and construction was supervised by Galveston architect Nicholas Clayton from

Merchant, banker and philanthropist George Sealy built the Open Gates for his wife and family in 1899. It was the center of commercial and social life in Galveston for numerous years. The Open Gates was used as a place of refuge during the 1900 Storm, sheltering as many as four hundred people. It is now part of the University of Texas Medical Branch (UTMB) at Galveston and is used as a conference center. *Author's collection.*

1887 to 1889. At the time, Clayton was intimately familiar with the surrounding properties, having designed the original John Sealy hospital, called Old Red, and the carriage house for Open Gates. Sealy had moved to Texas in 1857 from Wilkes-Barre, Pennsylvania, to work at Ball, Hutchings and Company in Galveston, joining his brother John, and he later served as treasurer of the Gulf, Colorado and Santa Fe Railway. When it went bankrupt, Sealy bought it at foreclosure. His reorganization resulted in the new towns of Rosenberg, Sealy and Temple being developed along the route and named after officers of the railway.

Open Gates became the center of commercial and social life on the island for years. Additionally, the home was used as a refuge by as many as four hundred people during the peak of the 1900 Storm—despite taking on fifteen feet of water in the basement. In 1979, the Sealy family donated the home to the University of Texas Medical Branch (UTMB) at Galveston. Today, it serves UTMB as the Open Gates Conference Center, hosting a variety of meetings, seminars and receptions.

Texas Heroes Monument
Broadway and Rosenberg Avenue

The Texas Heroes Monument is another marker of Henry Rosenberg's love for the Galveston community. Commissioned by Rosenberg, the monument was designed to commemorate those who fought during the Texas Revolution. Constructed by the New England Granite Works, using granite and bronze, and sculpted by Louis Amateis, the monument cost $50,000 and was shipped in the spring of 1899 before being erected and unveiled on April 22, 1900. The monument stands seventy-four feet in height, including the bronze statue of Victory topping the statue's base, which is thirty-four feet in diameter. Victory holds a sheathed sword, entwined with roses, with her right hand extended and holding a crown of laurels.

Four massive columns make up the main portion of the monument and are carved out of a single block of granite; at the top of each are the words *patriotism*, *honor*, *devotion* and *courage*, each representing different qualities held by those who fought in the Revolution. Patriotism faces north, overlooking the entrance to Galveston (which would have also been considered the entrance to Texas). At the base is Sam Houston, flanked by representations of peace and war, above reliefs of Henry Smith, Edward Burleson, Ben Milam, James Fannin and James Bonham, with an additional bas relief of the Battle of San Jacinto. Courage, facing east, honors the Goliad Massacre. Honor faces west and honors those who died at the Battle of San Jacinto but never had photos made for memorialization; a bas relief commemorates Santa Anna's surrender. Devotion faces south and features Stephen F. Austin, who is surrounded by David Burnet, Davy Crockett, Frank Johnson, "Deaf" Smith and William Travis, along with a bas relief commemorating the fall of the Alamo.

Galveston City Hall
823 Rosenberg Avenue

This behemoth of a building was constructed in 1916, right at the end of the City Beautiful movement. The City Commission moved the offices of the municipal government to this large city hall building on Rosenberg. C.D. Hill & Company, out of Dallas, based their building on the Italian Renaissance palazzo, a favorite model at the time for office buildings. A public auditorium was originally built at the back of the building; it was damaged during Hurricane Carla in 1961 and then demolished, replaced by a new central fire station. The new fire station, unfortunately, led to the demise of the old fire station, then being housed in the remnants of Alfred Muller's City Hall and Market House from 1888.

Moody Mansion
2618 Broadway

The thirty-one-room, five-bathroom Moody Mansion, also known as the Willis-Moody Mansion, was completed in 1895 following its commissioning by Galveston socialite Narcissa Willis in 1893. Her husband had refused to build her dream home, hoping to distribute his liquid assets to his children on his death. When he died in 1892, Narcissa had other plans. She tore down her house and began plans for this mansion, causing her estrangement from her family until her passing in 1899. Willis lived alone in the house, her children never visiting the home, with only a single housekeeper.

English architect William H. Tyndall designed the mansion using elements from different cultures and periods, leading to an eclectic appearance. For the interior of the home, Willis employed Pottier & Stymus, a prominent New York furniture and design firm of the time whose client

The four-story palace known as Moody Mansion was completed in 1895 for Galveston socialite Narcissa Willis. William Lewis Moody Jr., a prominent financier and entrepreneur in the cotton business, bought the home in 1900 after a number of bidders dropped out following the 1900 storm. Moody family members lived here until 1986, when it was turned into a museum. *Author's collection.*

list included President Ulysses S. Grant, Thomas Edison and William Rockefeller. When Narcissa died, her daughter Beatrice put the home up for sale. Libbie Moody lived nearby and asked her husband, William Lewis Moody Jr., to put in a bid for the home. When the 1900 Storm struck, it upended the sale, with many of the bidders pulling out. The Moodys won the sale, spending only $20,000 of the home's $100,000 value to get the home. The couple moved their four children in, celebrating their first Christmas there in 1900.

Members of the Moody family lived in the mansion until 1986, when the home was transformed into a historic home museum commemorating the Moody family. When Hurricane Ike struck the island in September 2008, the Moody Mansion's basement flooded, leading to the loss of Libbie's potting room and the home's period kitchen. Since the basement space reopened in July 2014, it has housed the Galveston Children's Museum.

Betty Head Oleander Garden Park
2624 Sealy Avenue

Betty Head was Galveston's beautifier. Best known for her work in the International Oleander Society, Head was the prime force in establishing a permanent place to share the beauty of Galveston's official flower, the oleander. Brought to the island first in 1841 from Jamaica by Joseph Osterman, the beautiful but deadly ornamental plant was planted throughout the island city following the 1900 Storm. The island's landscape had been devastated, and this was a first step toward repairing its image. The plant, coupled with Galveston's soil and climate, became a great match. The International Oleander Society maintains this small park where visitors can find many colorful varieties of the plant.

Galveston Federal Building
601 Twenty-Fifth Street

The U.S. Post Office and Courthouse, also known as the Galveston Federal Building, serves as the federal court for the Galveston Division of the United States District Court for the Southern District of Texas. A rarity in Galveston, this eight-story 1937 Art Deco federal building is one of the few in this architectural style on the island. Clad in porous fossiliferous limestone, this rock is typical of coastal areas, and at that time, it was common to use materials quarried regionally whenever possible. This building was constructed on the site of an older post office and federal building, which was demolished to make room for the new iteration.

Originally, the building housed the post office on the first floor; postal inspectors on the second; various government offices on the third floor; the Customs Department on the fourth floor; petit and grand jury space on the fifth floor; judges, U.S. marshals, U.S. attorneys and a ceremonial courtroom on the sixth floor; and the cotton-classifying rooms and the Bureaus of Navigation and Agriculture on the seventh floor.

For some time, the Galveston Weather Bureau office was located here, from 1946 through 1995. When its offices were destroyed during the 1900 Storm, the bureau moved to the Trust Building and then, finally, to this location before leaving for League City on the mainland. Shortly after the installation of one of a nationwide system of weather surveillance radars, the one in Galveston, located here, became the backbone of severe weather detection along the Gulf of Mexico for more than thirty years. It became the site of the first live television broadcast of a hurricane, by CBS's Dan Rather—a native Houstonian—who reported on Hurricane Carla striking the Texas coast in September 1961. While the weather service has moved, the building still houses many federal offices.

Central Wharf
102 Kempner Street

At the foot of Twenty-First Street, Peter J. Menard built a wharf in 1840, joining in on much of early Galveston's waterfront development and activity. His property included the ground in front of three waterfront lots, running from the bayfront to the boundary line, with wharf privileges—essentially being given the property by the Galveston City Company in exchange for the promise to build a wharf. Until these flats were filled in, water from the bay came right up to the Strand at Twenty-First Street, while wooden trestles on pilings reached out to the nine-foot channel. Ships entering the port were limited due to sand bars and depth; even lighting had to be provided in order to bring cargo and passengers into Galveston, the latter of which generally had to walk on wooden planks to wade their way to the Strand.

Menard's was the third wharf in the city. It came to be called Central Wharf because of its location. When the flats were eventually filled in, the wharves were moved out to meet the channel, and Central Wharf was

Seen here in an 1845 drawing, the Port of Galveston has been active since 1825, when it was part of Mexico. It is located on the eastern end of the island, stretching 9.3 miles from the open gulf. The port consists of the Galveston Ship Channel, the south side of Pelican Island, the north side of the island and the entrance to Galveston Bay. *Courtesy of the Library of Congress.*

renamed Pier 21. In 1854, the Galveston wharves were consolidated under the present Wharf Company. By this point, ships, schooners, steamboats and other small boats could land here, and prior to the completion of the railroad, all cargo for Houston steamboats was delivered at this wharf. The famous 1877 barque *Elissa* is now berthed here for viewing, touring and maritime exhibits, while Fisherman's Wharf provides a seafood market.

Interurban Line Remnants
Throughout the Island

The Galveston-Houston Electric Railway opened on the island in 1911. Running from downtown Houston to downtown Galveston and back, it operated from 1911 until 1936. Throughout the state, the electric interurban industry totaled nearly five hundred miles and contained the second-largest interurban milage west of the Mississippi, with nearly 20 percent of it located in the Houston-Galveston and Beaumont-Port Arthur areas. During its years of operation, the Galveston-Houston Electric Railway Company ran fifty miles between the two cities. During 1925 and 1926, it won first place in the nation in an interurban speed contest. The popularity of automobiles and burgeoning airline traffic eventually led to the demise of the line. A handful of tracks can still be seen throughout Galveston, and a streetcar now operates in and around the Strand and downtown.

Kuhn's Wharf
102 Twentieth Street

Kuhn's Wharf was one of the island's first, and likely the most essential, wharf during Galveston's founding. The wharf, which was built between 1838 and 1839, extended from Eighteenth to Twentieth Street along Galveston Bay. Texas Ranger Colonel Ephraim McLean had been granted wharf privileges by the Galveston City Company, provided he started construction of a wharf posthaste. This was the result.

The four-hundred-foot wharf became home to steamships, schooners and large ships, all imperative to the growth of both Galveston and Texas. However, shortly after building the wharf, McLean left to fight on the frontier. While he returned periodically, in his absence, the wharf began to deteriorate. Eventually, William Hendley Co., shipowners, and J.C. Kuhn,

Left: John Bankhead Magruder was a career military officer. He holds the distinction of having served in the armies of three nations: he was a U.S. Army officer in the Mexican-American War, a Confederate general and a postbellum general in the Imperial Mexican Army of Emperor Maximilian I. As a major general in the Civil War, he recaptured Galveston in 1863 for the Confederacy. *Courtesy of the Library of Congress.*

Below: The Mosquito Fleet consists of about seventy-five shrimp boats, named for their insect-like profiles. You can find them located at Pier 20, at the foot of Twentieth Street. Today, some boats are motored and others are sailboats with auxiliary power, and they shrimp or fish around the island and far south, leaving the harbor between midnight and dawn. They return near sunset, followed by flocks of seagulls. *Author's collection.*

Mosquito Fleet, Galveston, Texas.

a local merchant and cotton factor, acquired the wharf, improving the area. When Texas seceded from the Union in 1861, Kuhn sold his property on the Strand, his residence and all interests in the wharf before leaving for Europe as Confederates took control of the town.

The wharf then became the site of one of Texas's largest battles of the Civil War, the Battle of Galveston. On October 4, 1862, U.S. Navy ships entered the harbor, with Commander William B. Renshaw demanding Galveston's surrender. On October 8, a detachment of Federal troops landed on Kuhn's Wharf, marched to the Customs House and raised the Union flag. Throughout the Union's presence on the island, 350 men of the Forty-Second Massachusetts Regiment occupied the wharf, tore up the approach and erected a barricade about one hundred feet from the Strand and a similar one at the end of the wharf. They remained entrenched there until January 1, 1863, when Confederate major general John B. Magruder put his plan to recapture the city into effect.

Early that morning, Magruder's Confederate "Cotton Clads" (the superstructures had been removed and the ships bulwarked with cotton bales) slipped into the bay, troops moved into position around the approach to Kuhn's Wharf and the Union was attacked. When the Confederates captured the Federal ship *Harriet Lane*, the Federal forces lost their way of escape and their hopes of being supplied with reinforcements and surrendered. The wharf continued to operate following their capture.

The wharf is still abuzz with activity, however. At Pier 19, the Mosquito Fleet gathers. These shrimping boats earned their moniker due to their insect-like profiles. As many as 150 boats at a time find themselves jockeying for dock space, carrying cargoes of fruits and vegetables, poultry and game, fish and oysters and even building materials. These boats were the lifeblood of bringing supplies to the island until a wagon bridge was constructed to tie the mainland in with the island. Today, the fleet consists of both shrimp and charter boats. Nearby are a number of restaurants, charter boats and the Strand.

Stewart Building
222 Twenty-Second Street

Second-generation owners of a commission firm that was established in 1842, Julius Kauffman and Julius Runge hired architect Eugene T. Heiner to design this Italian Renaissance Revival–style building, completed in

1882. Kauffman-Runge housed commodities on the building's ground floor, with offices above. At that time, the firm was known as the world's foremost cotton exporter and was the initiator of coffee imports from Brazil. Its reputation brought many highly respected firms on the island to have an office in this building.

Maco Stewart bought the property in 1905, redesigning the interior. The building now featured a gallery effect with an arched skylight on the top floor. In 1908, Stewart founded Stewart Title Guaranty Company, which would become the largest title firm in Texas, and throughout its expansion across the country, it continuously held offices here. Since then, Stewart Title Guaranty Company has restored the building to its former splendor, including replacing an ornate cornice that had been missing since the 1900 Storm.

Galveston Ice & Cold Storage Building
104 Twenty-First Street

Sitting behind the oldest remaining commercial building in Galveston, the Hendley Building, are the remnant smokestacks and building of the Texas Ice & Cold Storage Company, constructed in 1910. The company was designed to produce over seventy tons of ice per day out of this reinforced concrete structure with a brick façade. The St. Louis firm of Widman and Walsh provided the Victorian design for the entire complex. Following the 1978 demolition of most of the structure, which once took up the rest of the block, its smokestack was donated to the Galveston Historical Foundation. The remaining three-story building, with its primary entrance on Twenty-First Street, features a railed balcony and a rectangular parapet extending above the flat roof. Today the building contains the Harborside Lofts and sports a mural on its west wall featuring penguins and polar bears, painted in 1989 by Lisa Hulquist.

Peanut Butter Warehouse
100 Twentieth Street

Located on the very edge of the Strand is the large concrete warehouse building known as the Peanut Butter Warehouse. The wood floors have long since been weathered by time, and a heavy brown wooden door sill

Today filled with lofts, an event space, bars and restaurants, and boutiques, the Peanut Butter Warehouse has been in use since 1895. Originally, the warehouse stored coffee beans, candy and peanut butter. Many of the original features of the building, such as a vintage Otis freight elevator, can still be found. *Author's collection.*

guards the entrance to the building. The Peanut Butter Warehouse has been in operation since 1895. Raised on platforms, the warehouse managed to weather the 1900 Storm, its platforms likely saving both the building and the warehouse's contents. The painted advertisement on the building also mentions that the building once stored chocolate, coffee and popcorn in addition to peanut butter. The building still contains an old Otis freight elevator and the raised wooden platform on the second story that was used for the tram car. The tram car ran along the rails, product was placed inside and then the car was taken to the elevator, where it was sent downstairs. The historic warehouse now contains shops, restaurants and bars, and serves as a luxury mid-rise loft building.

Chapter 2
THE LINE

Located near downtown, the Line was Galveston's red-light district. The madams here—generally agreed to be a stretch along Postoffice Street between Twenty-Fifth and Twenty-Ninth Streets—were among the very few operators on the island not required to pay some kind of kickback to the Maceo family. However, the madams had the good sense to forbid the act of gambling in their houses, hoping to keep the Maceos at bay.

In the years prior to World War II, gambling, prostitution and violations of the state's alcoholic beverage code were well known, and while the code was not strictly enforced, establishments tended to keep this kind of operation under wraps. However, Galveston was different. The red-light district here very well could have been the only one in the country at the time not only to thrive but also to do so with the blessings of both city hall—and the Catholic church. It has been estimated that it was the largest such district, proportionally speaking, in the world. For every sixty-two Galvestonians, there was one hooker, outranking places like Shanghai two to one and Chicago and Paris by more than seven to one. Vice wasn't even shied away from; police commissioner Walter Johnson once bragged that he was on the payroll of forty-six whorehouses, and Frank Biaggne, the county sheriff from 1933 to 1957, once explained to the state that he never raided the Balinese Room because it was a private club and he wasn't a member.

Only a few reminders remain of the Line. Some are nondescript, much like their madams intended them to be. Others are a little less so. Venture inside one brothel location, listed here in a bit, and you'll find remnants like notch marks among the items for sale in the room.

Mollie Walters Boardinghouse
2528 Postoffice Street

This is the famous boardinghouse built by Mollie Walters in 1886. Wrapping around the corner of Postoffice, this two-story wooden home features two interior chimneys and attached porches on both the first and second floors. Unfortunately, time has taken away many of this boardinghouse's contemporaries, and it is one of the few remnants of the famous red-light district. It was placed on the National Register of Historic Places in August 1984.

Mother Harvey's House
2528 Postoffice Street

The premier house on the island, Mother Harvey's sits on the popular 2500 block of Postoffice, considered the busiest part of the red-light district. During the 1940s, an era when prostitution and other vices thrived and were essential cogs in Galveston's economy, it has been estimated that houses like Mother Harvey's earned between $15,000 and $20,000 a week.

The Rainbow Room
116 Twentieth Street

Downtown brothels that found themselves within Galveston's business district and outside the Line were typically two-story buildings. They featured a large main entrance into a bar or a restaurant on the ground floor. Typically, there was a side door, hidden from view, that opened onto a set of stairs leading to the second story brothel rooms. You could find them in the city directory; there would be a slight change in name or address in order to differentiate between the legitimate business and the entrance to the brothel. The Rainbow Room is one such example; the nightclub was listed at 114 Twentieth Street; but the Rainbow Room, with its odd little side door, had an address two digits higher.

Former Brothel
3311 Ball Street

This home on Ball Street was built specifically to be used as a brothel. Currently a residence, it was constructed in the Line's later years. The home is definitely starting to show its age; however, it continues to stand, while its neighbors of ill repute have all been taken away.

Havana Alley Cigar Shop and Lounge Building
201 Twenty-Sixth Street

What is now the Havana Alley Cigar Shop and Lounge once operated as a brothel. It was disguised as a hotel and operated in this location until the early 1990s.

Alibi Bar Building
2325 Church Street

The Alibi Bar, formerly the Wizzard, is a dive bar. Not pretty, kind of cool, and the drinks are cold. The building, in its early days, also served as a brothel. When it was constructed, the building featured a legitimate business downstairs and a brothel upstairs.

Oleander Hotel
423 Twenty-Fifth Street

When Scott and Holly Hanson purchased the century-old former Oleander Hotel, little did they know the historical surprise hidden at the top of a rotting staircase, sealed off for decades. The Hansons were opening their business Antique Warehouse in the space. Upstairs, they found that the unused second floor contained twenty-eight rooms—ones where prostitutes once offered their services.

The couple knew that Postoffice once was the heart of Galveston's red-light district, so they had some inkling that the upstairs might have a similar story to some of the other buildings of vice but were not so certain—until they met "Jack," a man who had been homeless at the age of six in 1933.

When the Hansons bought the century-old Oleander Hotel to open their business Antique Warehouse, little did they know what they would find on the unused second floor. Upstairs were twenty-eight rooms where prostitutes once plied their trade. The location was in the Line, a stretch of dozens of brothels (fifty-five in 1929). Red lights, tally marks on walls and equipment were all left behind. *Author's collection.*

The brothel's madam took pity on Jack, letting him live in a closet in return for doing chores and running errands. Jack told the Hansons that the clients would enter from the alley and be taken up a flight of stairs to the drawing room to meet the women. Each room had a red light hanging over the door to signal "in use," and in at least one room, there are penciled tally marks on the wall. Transom windows above the doors were tilted just so and used by the madam to monitor her girls.

Queen Laura's Bordello
2528 Postoffice Street

Formerly known as the Mollie Walters House, this home was built for use as a female boardinghouse. Located in Galveston's red-light district and constructed in 1886, this two-story home contained fifteen rooms and, while listed as a "female boarding house," was well known on the Line as a bordello.

Hall-Scott, Levi and Hughes Buildings
2501–2503, 2509–2511 and 2513–2515 Market Street

This row of buildings is bookended with two designed by George B. Stowe: the Hall-Scott and Hughes Buildings from 1906 and 1907, respectively. The middle building, the Levi, was constructed about a decade later. Stowe designed the first two for a series of investors. Rehabilitation of the Levi Building in 1996 reconstructed a long-lost sidewalk canopy. This part of the district was off-limits to the middle-class White women and girls of Galveston. This area of the Line was also called the Restricted District, a segment designed to combine the vice of Galveston with businesses, no matter how mundane, for African Americans and immigrants. The vice activities lasted, and were tolerated, well into the mid-twentieth century, when they were pushed underground.

George Washington Carver Theater/Teatro Ray
2523 Market Street

Giosue Martini, a Galveston theater entrepreneur, built both this theater and another one, the now-destroyed Booker T. Theater at 2601 Market, located farther down the Line. Both were constructed in 1948 to serve African American audiences. In addition to this area hosting the Line, these blocks also served as the business and entertainment district for African American and Mexican American islanders.

Madam Mary "Gouch-Eye" Russel's Bordello (a.k.a. The 27 Club) 2710 Postoffice Street

Madam Russel ran the bordello that once sat on this now-empty lot. Most of the homes in this area, back in the 1920s, looked similar to the house to the left. Rumor has it that whenever the mayor needed a special girl for a visiting bigwig coming to the island, he would go directly to Madam Russel. The gratitude would be returned; she got tipped off to law enforcement house raids. Supposedly, those were mostly only for show. The thought at the time in Galveston was that, within the boundaries of the Line, bordellos served the johns, thereby keeping prostitution off the streets. This open period on the island peaked in the 1940s. Some of the bordellos could earn as much as $20,000 in one week; adjusted for inflation, that amount is roughly $420,000 today.

Chapter 3

THE FACTORY AND WAREHOUSE DISTRICT

This district was established on the island in the late 1800s. A hub for the cotton trade in the region, it became home to several large cotton warehouses where cotton from throughout Texas was stored before shipment to other parts of the United States and the world. As the port and the city expanded, the heart of the district migrated but remains centered on this area.

This port has been significant to the United States, the Confederacy, the Republic of Texas and entities before them as a hub for international trade and commerce. Ships carrying goods from nearly every country imaginable could be found docking here. Originally, Galveston used to ship primarily cotton and agricultural goods. Millions of dollars were invested into cotton expiration, compression and storage. In fact, development of the railroad in Galveston revolutionized this trade both in Texas and throughout the region, making long-distance transportation of cotton by rail economically feasible. Eventually, the island became a major hub for other commodities.

Remnants remain of the old district. Warehouses, even historic ones, can still be found between Twenty-Eighth Street and Fifty-First Street north of Broadway. This was a natural extension of the Port of Galveston, especially as cotton became king of the South. Today, warehouses can still be found, historic and repurposed, still being used or waiting for reuse. Much of the traffic in this area is now cruise related, but its old historic purpose has yet to dissipate.

GH&H, IG&N and MK&T Freight Office
325 Thirty-Third Street

Constructed following the Storm of 1900, the Galveston, Houston & Henderson Railroad, along with two other corporations, built this freight depot. This was originally the site of GH&H's first rail station, predating track extensions into the downtown wharves in the 1870s. The company previously, in 1860, had bridged Galveston Bay, beginning service between Galveston and Houston for the first time.

The depot is built of orange-red brick, and its cast ornamentation and inset limestone loggia give it the look of a civic building. As to why you see three front doors to the structure, they were not part of a redesign project. Instead, there was one for each of the railway lines that occupied the space inside. A long and canopied loading dock stretches out behind the station.

The GH&H Freight Depot was built in 1904 and jointly owned by the Missouri-Kansas-Texas ("Katy") Railroad and the International & Great Northern Railroad. Both relied on the GH&H line to deliver goods between Houston and Galveston. *Author's collection.*

Galveston Water & Electric Light Station
3002 Ball Street

Designed by Galveston architect Charles William Bulger, this red brick station building was constructed in 1904. Its predecessor, a pump station erected in 1889, was destroyed in the 1900 Storm, leaving behind only the buff limestone foundation, on which the newer building was erected. Bulger's design fits the civic purpose of this building, recalling the baths of Rome with its arched windows and pressed metal cornice. Originally, the building consisted of two rooms, one for the electric generator and the other for the water pumps. The floor, now filled in and sealed, once contained pits housing the water pumps that supplied island residents and visitors with drinking water until the 2000s.

In 2020, the City of Galveston and the Texas General Land Office, along with the LaBiche Architectural Group, rehabilitated the building as a community center for the neighborhood. Elements from the original pump station—including equipment, signage, one of the original 1889 water tanks and hardware—were left on display to interpret the history of the building.

Wesley Tabernacle United Methodist Church
902 Twenty-Eighth Street

The African American Methodist community dates back to 1848 on the island. Then, Gail Borden deeded land on Broadway for the construction of a church for enslaved people. Following the Civil War, the congregation changed its affiliation from Methodist Episcopal Church, South, to African Methodist Episcopal. In 1867, the church became known as Reedy Chapel AME. The St. Paul Methodist Episcopal Church split from Reedy Chapel, and in 1868, the St. Paul group divided, with one group organizing in 1869 as an independent congregation under Reverend Peter Cavanaugh.

Early parishioners would meet in a one-room house located on Broadway between Thirty-Eighth and Thirty-Ninth Street, but as the church grew, this location was purchased and that one-room house was moved to this site. The congregation lost church buildings in both the 1879 fire and the 1900 Storm, and a new one-story building was constructed in their place. In 1924, the church building was remodeled, the building raised and a new first floor constructed, giving the building a combination of architectural styles, including Gothic Revival and Craftsman. Inside, the pews and the altar furniture date to the 1881 sanctuary. The church served as the home of the first female African American Methodist minister, the Reverend Perrie Joy Jackson, in the 1960s.

Central High School
3014 Sealy Avenue

Now Central Middle School, when built in 1954, it was complemented on Avenue O with Ball High School. Central replaced an earlier school of the same name that was located at Twenty-Seventh and Avenue M as the public high school for African American students. The building's design, by Preston M. Gerne and R.R. Rapp, out of Fort Worth, intentionally nearly mirrors that of Ball. The school takes over a two-block swath and sits atop what once was the site of the nineteenth-century Gulf City Cotton Press.

Central High School, the first for African American students in Texas, was originally named the Central Colored School when it opened in 1885. From 1886 to 1967, when it consolidated with Ball High School, more than forty thousand students attended classes, graduating more than seven thousand students. This building was the school's second and would become the Old Center Cultural Center in 1973. *Author's collection.*

Wright Cuney Park/USO Building
718 Forty-First Street

Born into slavery near Hempstead, Texas, in May 1846, Norris Wright Cuney was an American politician, businessman, union leader and civil rights activist. Following the Civil War, he became active in Galveston politics, serving as both an alderman and a national Republican delegate. In 1889, he was appointed United States collector of customs in Galveston. Wright Cuney had the highest-ranking appointed position of any African American in the late nineteenth-century South. He also established his own business of stevedores, helped unionize Black workers in Galveston and helped attract Black voters to the still-new Republican Party. Due to his influence, he improved the lives of Blacks in the city through employment and educational opportunities.

Norris Wright Cuney was born into slavery in 1846 but forged a career in post–Civil War Texas that is unmatched. He settled in Galveston following the Civil War, gaining experience and sway while holding several civic offices in the city and county and becoming the Republican Party's national committeeman from Texas in 1886. His experience and wealth improved the lives of formerly enslaved people in Texas. *Author's collection.*

Wright Cuney eventually rose to chair of the Texas Republican Party and became a national committeeperson. He is considered the most important Black leader in Texas during the nineteenth century and one of the most important in United States history. The City of Galveston, in 1937, established Wright Cuney Park in honor of Norris Wright Cuney. The recreation center building was constructed in 1941 to serve as the USO building. Also located here is the *Guitar* tree sculpture created by local sculptor Earl Jones.

Cotton Concentration Company Sheds
5402–5628 Broadway

Cotton was a hot commodity in nineteenth- and twentieth-century Galveston. George Sealy Jr. organized the Cotton Concentration Company to merge with the Galveston Wharf Company, of which he was president. The company's sheds were constructed in 1928 and are covered by three-block-long concrete walls, broken only by an interspersed set of gateways and beautified by palms and bougainvillea. The sheds themselves are each four blocks deep and run back to Church Street but have sat vacant since the 1980s.

Falstaff Brewery Building
3300 Church Street

Built in 1895, the Falstaff Brewery Complex was originally one of Adolphus Busch's regional brewery projects as his company expanded throughout the United States. The brewery, despite changing hands several times during its life, operated for more than eighty years. After spending years standing vacant, in 2018, two components of the complex were rehabilitated for use as long-term cruise ship parking and a storage facility. Developers have made plans in the past that included a boutique hotel, a gymnasium and an eatery. The building remains one of the last standing factories in this district.

Jack Johnson Tree Sculpture
4402 North Live Oaks Circle

The Jack Johnson Tree Sculpture is located within the Oaks subdivision. There are a few parking spaces in front of the small neighborhood green space where the sculpture permanently sits. Galveston native Arthur John "Jack" Johnson, noted elsewhere in this book, became the first African American world heavyweight boxing champion, grew up on the East Side and honed his fighting skills through matches while working on the Galveston Wharves. When Ike swept across the island, thirty thousand trees were destroyed or damaged, some by the wind but most by the standing saltwater. This sculpture was created by artist Earl Jones, who completed it in 2011. Over the years, it was subject to exposure to both time and the elements but also ants and termites. Local artist, boxing fan and business owner Rick Morrison took on the deteriorating nature of the sculpture in 2017. His preservation work of this site was finished in August 2020.

Chapter 4

THE EAST END

This section contains the area of, and immediately in the vicinity of, Galveston's East End Historic District. The historic district, which has been placed on the National Register of Historic Places and has been awarded the designation of National Historic Landmark, has very definitive boundaries. I've included some additional properties in the chapter that are outside of the district boundaries but that I think you will find interesting regardless.

The architecture of the East End is truly the highlight of this section. At one time, this was an area of blight and decay. In recent history, the neighborhood has transformed itself into a vibrant, desirable one. Along these streets, you will find a variety of architectural styles and periods, the earliest being that of the Greek Revival style, which was common during the 1850s. The homes represent a vast spectrum of sizes, ranging from small and simple cottages to large, elaborate, castle-like palaces. The homes on the East End are standing reminders of the "Gilded Age" in Galveston's history, some of which have survived moves, fires, floods and hurricanes.

Located adjacent to the East End Historic District is the rest of the East End Flats and the campus of the University of Texas Medical Branch. When it began operating in 1845, the Galveston City Hospital was tucked away in the far northeast corner of the city, located around Ninth Street and Strand. This was, at the time, as far away from the city center as one could feel potentially safe—at least with the time's understanding of health standards and the fear that traveled with them. In 1881, Galveston

The original portion of the George Manor was constructed in 1851. Since that time, it's been expanded and has changed ownership several times. During the 1900 Storm, Ida Austin and her niece saw the encroaching waters from the gulf, opened the doors to the house and let the water flow through, filling the rooms with three feet of water. Today, it serves as a luxury B&B. *Author's collection.*

was chosen as the location for the Medical Department of the University of Texas, and what followed was a shift in development on the island. What once was on the fringe of society in Galveston is today the center of the Galveston community. Blocks were committed for development at the end of Eighth Street when it opened in 1891. Beyond this were the Flats, marshy lowland that was undesirable for building but great for fishing and hunting.

By the 1940s, a lot of the Flats was being filled in to make way for eastward development on the island. The Groesbeck grid from the original town plan was extended east to what was then an imaginary First Street. Today, numerous University of Texas Medical Branch and associated buildings abound, including the Moody Medical Library Building, the Shriners Hospital for Crippled Children Galveston Burns Institute and multiple other medical buildings housing operations from the 1960s to the present.

Island City Woodworking Company Warehouse
1801–1803 Mechanic Street

The Island City Woodworking company was established by Galveston builder Mills C. Bowden. Despite its construction date of 1908, this building, which covers a quarter-block just outside the Strand, is exemplary of the nineteenth-century makeup of this part of Galveston: artisans' shops and warehouses. Still evident on the exterior is the name of the company, starting to fade into its role as a ghost sign as the years stretch on.

Cottage Home
1428 Mechanic Street

No date of construction has been identified for this home, nor has its architect. However, one attractive feature of Galveston's nineteenth-century cottage homes was that they were relatively simple to move from one lot to another. The act was actually so common on the island that the *Galveston Daily News* reported on it in 1884, calling the practice a "house moving nuisance." While the original location of this home is debated, it appears that the place where it sits on its current plot of land once served as the neighbors' side yard.

Rosenberg House
1306 Market Street

This 1859 Italianate villa was built by Swiss immigrant Henry Rosenberg, who became a successful merchant and land investor and, eventually, the island's largest benefactor. The home stood out amid the Civil War–era wooden cottages around it. Many of the materials were imported from Switzerland. The home sports a rooftop cupola and a single-story veranda topped with a balcony. Inside are eight marble fireplaces, tall wall mirrors and a hand-carved plaster ceiling. Galveston's great benefactor, Rosenberg, gave the city funds to construct fountains, a public library, schools, an orphanage, a home for elderly women and a YMCA. In 1990, the house was purchased by the Sealy Smith Foundation, which restored the home for use as a conference center and guest home for the University of Texas Medical Branch.

The Original Mexican Cafe is the longest continually operating restaurant on the island still at is original location. Located on the corner of Fourteenth and Market, it opened in 1916 and is a consistent winner of awards for its food and margaritas. *Author's collection.*

The Original Mexican Cafe
1401 Market Street

Founded by Ramon Guzman in 1916, the Original Mexican Cafe opened in this existing building in 1921. Ramon, born in Mexico in 1883, immigrated to the United States in 1903. Downstairs was the cafe, while Ramon and his wife, Hattie, whom he married around 1913, lived upstairs. Ramon ran the business until his death in 1933. Hattie maintained ownership of the café until her death in 1951. Despite a change in ownership over the years since, the café continues to provide islanders and visitors alike with great Tex-Mex recipes. The restaurant is continually ranked as one of the Best of Galveston County in multiple food categories. It stands as the longest continually operating restaurant on the island.

1885 Fire Homes
1600 Block of Market Street

Picking any one of these homes along the 1600 block of Market makes sense historically. All these homes were built following 1886 to replace the homes that had been destroyed on this block during the November 13, 1885, conflagration. The home at 1614 Market Street serves as a good example of these homes, as does its neighbors.

Bohn and Neuwiller Building
1801–1805 Market Street

These two identical buildings represent a spillover from the workshop district to the north and east to the more residential district to the south and west. The corner building, 1801 Market, contains George Bohn's sheet iron, tinware, hardware and crockery business. Next door, at 1805, is the Neuwiller building, with its stucco-faced exterior. Charles F. Neuwiller operated his cabinet shop downstairs while he had residential quarters upstairs, as did Bohn. These two buildings have perpetuated the standard downtown loft building type.

Great A&P Tea Company
1127 Postoffice Street

Most of the corner stores you will find in the residential neighborhoods in Galveston tend to be boxy, two-story and wooden with low-pitched roofs. Sometimes, a few ornamental flourishes can be located, but for the most part, they're fairly similar. This A&P corner store deviates from that plan. Its design, influenced by the Craftsman style, fits in more seamlessly with the homes in the neighborhood. Sitting atop a raised basement are the second-story front porch, casement windows and the outdoor stair, whose parapet acts as a separator to the family's residence up above.

Purity Ice Cream
1202 Postoffice Street

Built around 1878, this was originally the Purity Ice Cream Factory, the oldest ice cream manufacturer in Texas. These days, it serves as a residence, but the neon sign still sits out front. You can still get Purity Ice Cream in Galveston. One of the most historic locations serving this brand today is La King's Confectionary on the Strand. Purity, owned and operated by

G.B. Brynston, was so popular during its heyday that few drugstore soda fountains or grocery stores carried any other brand; even the public school cafeterias had single-cup servings.

800 Block of Church Street
806 and 810 Church Street

This block lay conveniently right outside the "area of total destruction" from the 1900 Storm and contains a number of homes that managed to survive the storm's impact. These homes from the nineteenth century, and those few from the early twentieth, showcase the more modest homes of the time on Galveston. As one heads toward the eastern end of the historic district, the trees begin to thin out. Here, as it was in other neighborhoods, the denser the tree cover, the higher the social prestige. In this part of town, the trees thin out. Small wooden houses filled out the 800 block of Church Street prior to 1900, but the storm that year devastated the area. Most of the homes built on this block, then, were either survivors or were moved into other areas of town.

The houses at 806 and 810 are indicative of the small, one-story Victorian cottages on the street. Real estate investor Henry Trueheart bought the three lots these two houses occupy. True to his promise, he rented the lots to African American tenants: Alfred Brown, Cato Fields and Mary James, all of whom owned their own houses. When this property was redeveloped, the tenants moved their homes to other rented sites, a common practice on the island at the time. Shotgun-style homes, tenant homes and Gulf Coast cottages can be found along this block.

William Werner Grocery Building
1401 Church Street

Built in 1859, the Werner Grocery Building is one of the oldest surviving corner stores in the city. Not only that, it's maintained its footprint here since it appeared in the 1871 C. Drie bird's-eye view of the island. Its corner-L plan, so the rear of the building opens along Fourteenth Street, allows the prevailing breeze to flow into its double galleries. A remodel in 1886 is likely when the twin projecting bay windows were added. In its latest iteration, the grocery store serves as a barbershop.

Darragh House Fences
519 Fifteenth Street

Now but a mere memory, the Darragh House was constructed in 1889 for John Darragh, the president of the Galveston Wharf Co., by Alfred Muller. The home was destroyed in 1990; however, the cast-iron fencing survived. Tile sidewalks lead visitors to the property, now a park that belongs to the East End Historical District Association.

Alleyway: Church and Winnie Streets
Alley Between 1500 Block of Church and 1500 Block of Winnie

The back alleys of Galveston aren't just there. No, they have a story to be told. In addition to the "front-street" residents, the city's neighborhoods typically had a sizable alley population as well. These secondary or service buildings, which were commonly situated near the alleys, were oriented to the front house and typically included slave or servant quarters. Rear homes that faced the alley were usually built as rental properties. Still to be found, this stretch of back alley homes is typically what you would find located on the north, or Church Street, side. On the south, or Winnie Street, side is a handful of service buildings, the only surviving examples of the kind that existed on that side. The alley buildings clearly reflected the socioeconomic status of the front-side residents.

Cherry House
1602 Church Street

Constructed for Wilbur Cherry, the founding publisher of the *Galveston News*, this home is one of the oldest in the East End Historical District. The style is very similar to that of the early wooden houses constructed in Galveston from the 1830s through the mid-1850s. This location, at Sixteenth Street, is where Church Street returned to the middle class. The Cherry House is one of only two homes in this neighborhood to escape the destructive nature of the disastrous 1885 fire.

King Vidor Home
1702 Winnie Avenue

King Wallis Vidor.
Courtesy of University of Washington Special Collections.

King Wallis Vidor was born into a well-off family in Galveston. His grandfather had emigrated from Hungary to Galveston in the early 1850s. This L-plan house was built in 1886 by King's father, Charles, for his family. King was born in the front downstairs bedroom and raised in this home. He was six years old when he witnessed the destruction of the 1900 Storm, using this experience to help push forward a career in writing and, more prominently, in film. In 1938, King Vidor was called on to direct the black-and-white scenes in *The Wizard of Oz*, including the cyclone scene. The movie's producer, and a good friend of Vidor's, David Selznick, was busy at the time finishing his epic *Gone With the Wind* when he called on Vidor's assistance.

The live oak in front of the Vidor home stood for years until Hurricane Ike came along. It has since gone under the hands of local artist Jim Phillips, who transformed the felled tree into the Tin Man and Toto from *The Wizard of Oz*, in an homage to King Vidor.

Boddeker Tenant House
902 Ball Avenue

Constructed in 1906 as an investment property by investor J.A. Boddeker, the cottage exemplifies two things about this area of Galveston. One is that the building represents the conservative nature of design and build at this time and also served as new construction for hurricane-destroyed homes from 1900. Additional homes can be found on this block in the L-fronted Victorian cottage design. This block, however, sat in the path of total destruction from the 1900 Hurricane. This cottage, and likely many others of the period, was constructed to replace earlier destroyed homes.

When philanthropist Henry Rosenberg died in May 1893, he left the bulk of his estate to fund various charitable projects. One of these included the installation of seventeen fountains, for use by both people and animals. Today, only nine of these exist; this one was removed from the middle of Twentieth Street and the Strand in 1949 and replaced here at the corner of Postoffice and Twenty-First Street in 1995. *Author's collection.*

Alderdice Park
1501 Ball Avenue

Alderdice Park was developed as a resting place for walkers by the East End Historical District Association. One of the fountains that Henry Rosenberg donated to "water man and beast" was moved to this location from Sixth and Broadway. Many others can be found at various locations throughout Galveston, including one of the more notable designs and locations at the corner of Postoffice and Twenty-First Street.

Trube Castle
1627 Sealy Avenue

Also known as the Danish Castle, Trube Castle was built in 1890 and is Alfred Muller's grandest surviving home. Built by John Trube, a former gardener in Denmark turned highly profitable realtor in Houston, this castle features a tower, although only mock in design. The front ramped staircase provides access to the surrounding black-and-white tiled sidewalks. Trube supposedly hired Muller to design his dream house and to thumb his nose at the island's conservative elite. The home is actually brick but covered with a rusticated finish, a mixture of crushed oyster shells, concrete and water, in order to appear like cut stone and, therefore, more castle-like.

Chancery Building, Diocese of Galveston
1411 Sealy Building

This 1924 Mission-style building served as the Chancery Office of the Diocese of Galveston and was commissioned by Bishop Byrne, who also bought the Gresham House, now known as the Bishop's Palace. Shortly after his purchase, the diocese placed this little office building on the block behind the Gresham House for its administrative offices.

Bondies-Robertson House
1212 Sealy Avenue

This house was built in 1877 for George Bondies as a two-story residence. In 1886, Joseph A. Robertson purchased the house, making multiple alterations from 1886 through 1904. This Victorian Eastlake home boasts one of the most ornate staircases in Galveston and includes a double gallery and a chamfered bay front that dominates the main façade of the home. Following the 1900 hurricane, numerous photographs were taken of the storm's destruction from the restored widow's walk. This location also has one of the famed Hurricane Ike tree sculptures. It is called *Gulf Titans* and features a swordfish, dolphins, fish and a large clamshell.

The Path of Total Destruction
1109 and 1110 Sealy Avenue

Where these two homes stand now was, in 1900, the beginning of the area of total destruction from the hurricane. The small house at 1110 Sealy was constructed in 1889 as part of the Alexander Allen homestead (his home is at 1118 Sealy) and remodeled in 1915 by W.L. Garbade, a later owner.

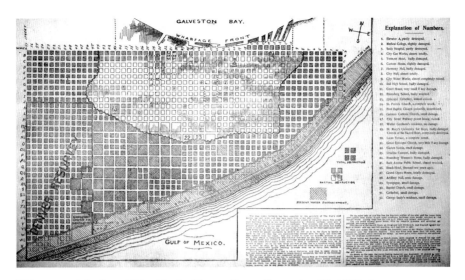

This map, originally published in the *Houston Post* on September 27, 1900, shows the destruction caused by the 1900 Storm. One can also see the location of water encroachment and the buildings or properties that suffered total or partially destruction. *Courtesy of the Library of Congress.*

Across the street at 1109 Sealy is the Colonial Revival–style house of dry goods merchant Henry C. Eiband.

Horace Scull Shotgun Houses
913 and 915 Sealy Avenue

This pair of 1901 shotgun houses lies within the blocks located east of the East End, ranging from Tenth to Seventh Streets (Sixth Street is where the tidal flats began). Following the Civil War, this area was developed as a lower income neighborhood, as it was not considered to be very desirable real estate; it was low-lying and prone to flooding. Here, surrounding these two homes, would have been where Galveston's lower-income Black and White families would settle and where African American institutions—schools and churches—were placed.

Unfortunately, this neighborhood was devastated during the 1900 Storm. Many of the more modest homes, and a considerable amount of lives, were lost. Following the storm, homes such as these twelve-foot-wide shotgun cottages served as new construction for the neighborhood but managed to keep it low-income. These two homes specifically were constructed by Horace

Scull, an African American carpenter and cabinetmaker. Additionally, Scull was a community builder, having organized some of the first schools for African American children in Galveston. His widow, Emily, and other members of Scull's family lived at 915 Sealy Avenue.

Commissary Houses
807 and 809 Sealy Avenue

Following the 1900 Storm, homes, of course, were not immediately available or rebuilt. During the transitory period following the storm, many of the shotgun houses earned the name "commissary house" because they were intended to serve as temporary housing for those left homeless following the storm. These two homes, constructed in 1908 and 1906 respectively, serve as reminders of that era. Here you will find homes that are small in size, with shuttered windows and very modest decorations. George Edwards built these two homes on the site of his house that was destroyed in the storm.

Sacred Heart Catholic Church
928 Fourteenth Street/1308 Broadway

Constructed of cast-in-place reinforced concrete in 1904 by a team of Jesuit lay brothers, Sacred Heart Catholic Church stands as a stark white sentinel on the island. Prior to this iteration, another Sacred Heart Church sat here. It was constructed by Nicholas Clayton in 1892 in the High Victorian Romanesque style, and it sat then where the rectory, built in 1925 by R.R. Rapp, is today, facing Broadway. It was destroyed by the 1900 Storm.

Brother Cornelius Otten SJ, who had previously worked with Clayton at Sacred Heart, was called in to build the new church. Ironically, Otten had taken Clayton's plans without permission and constructed a similar church—right down to size and scale—of the same design in Augusta, Georgia. Otten, along with Brother Peter Jiménez, a Spanish-born carpenter and architect, was called on to design the new building. His design, borrowed in part from previously constructed churches in Toledo, Spain, and New Orleans, Louisiana, had a heavy Moorish influence. The profiled onion dome, used to highlight the order's Spanish influence, was an alteration made in 1910–12 by Clayton, who replaced Jiménez's original, squatter dome.

Bishop's Palace
1402 Broadway

Built by Nicolas Clayton from 1887 to 1892 for Walter Gresham, the Galvestonian railroad investor, lawyer and politician, Bishop's Palace is likely Galveston's best-known building. It's almost like a fanfare of architectural features: richly colored, textured materials; gables, chimney stacks and towers—plus, it's very large. When it comes to who was keeping up with whom, Bishop's Palace was the standard-bearer, and it shows. It was built of Texas limestone, decorated with bands of gray and pink granite and red sandstone. When it was constructed, it cost a reported $125,000, an astronomical sum at a time when middle-income, two-story family houses were typically going for $2,000. It doesn't entirely stray from Clayton's other large-scale designs. One interesting feature of note is the conservatory, built to contain Mrs. Gresham's collection of specimen ferns. Overall, the home was designed to recall to others the stately mansions of England and the châteaux of France.

It was purchased in 1923 by the Catholic Diocese of Galveston and named the Bishop's Place. The only bishop to live there, though, was Reverend Christopher Byrne. Thirteen years following his death, in 1963, the diocese opened the house to the public as the first historic house museum on Broadway. It was purchased from the diocese in 2014 by the Galveston Historical Foundation.

Nicholas Clayton made a name for himself in Galveston as one of its most prominent architects during the Victorian era. Born in Ireland, he moved with his family to the United States in 1848. While he designed buildings throughout Texas and in a few other locations, many of his grandest island designs still stand, including Bishop's Palace, the Ashbel Smith Building and St. Patrick's Church. *Courtesy of the Library of Congress.*

Kempner House
1502 Broadway

This Neoclassical home was completed in 1906 but begun in 1904. Local architect Charles W. Bulger designed it for Isaac Herbert Kempner, a leading figure in Galveston's business community and, at the time, only twenty-one years old. Isaac's father, Harris, had immigrated to Galveston from Poland in 1894, becoming a leading businessman in his own right with interests in insurance, railroads, banking and cotton. Isaac, being the eldest of Harris's eight children, took over his father's multiple businesses.

In 1902, Isaac married Henrietta Blum, also a child of a prominent Galveston businessman. Following the 1900 Storm, Kempner stepped up and showed considerable civic leadership, helping lead the city's efforts in rebuilding the island's infrastructure, including this home, replete with colossal Corinthian columns and extensive art glass in the windows. Then, from 1917 to 1919, he served as Galveston's mayor. In 1924, architect John Staub expanded the structure west with a two-story concrete and stucco wing when more lots became available. The home remained in the Kempner family until 1970. Located nearby, at 1516 Broadway, is the Kempner Garage Apartment, constructed in 1940.

Saint Paul's Methodist Church
1427 Broadway

St. Paul's is one of the oldest African American churches on Galveston Island. The present church building was constructed to replace a building destroyed during the 1900 Storm. Built in 1902, this wood-frame church, designed by C.W. Bulger, is reminiscent of nineteenth-century churches. Bulger took his church and gave it a Victorian twist, featuring a corner tower, a spire and multiple side entrances.

Lucas Terrace Apartments
1407–1409 Broadway

The Lucas Terrace Apartments were reconstructed by owner and bricklayer Thomas Lucas, using salvaged materials, after the total destruction of the 1900 storm. He followed a "strictly modern English design."

Ashbel Smith Hall, UTMB
902–928 Strand Street

Nestled in the campus of the University of Texas Medical Branch (UMTB), you will find Texas's first medical school. As Galveston grew and business flourished, the island became a desired destination. However, its location also made it ripe for yellow fever outbreaks, regularly occurring events that would decimate Galveston's population. This brought a medical community to the island, led by Yale grad Dr. Ashbel Smith from Connecticut. Dr. Smith had written the first treatise on yellow fever in Texas in 1839 and used his experience and connections in politics to establish the Texas Medical College on the island in 1873. The first structure for the newly established college was named in honor of Dr. Smith, who had died five years prior to its construction.

The Romanesque Revival building was designed by Nicholas Clayton in 1890. The masonry is Texas sandstone, red pressed brick and granite—rendering its nickname, Old Red, perfect. The 1900 Storm laid waste to Clayton's original tall, tiered pavilion roof, located atop the central section of the building, which stood on what was then the edge of the island. When Clayton came to repair the building in 1901, this feature was not rebuilt. As a consequence, the design lost its original—more vertical than horizontal—appearance. It wasn't until 1923, when construction began on the medical laboratory building, that Old Red was joined with additional permanent academic structures.

The Ashbel Smith Building, also known as Old Red, was designed by Nicholas Clayton and constructed in 1891. It was the first building for the University of Texas Medical Branch. It was named, in 1949, for Ashbel Smith, a Republic of Texas diplomat and one of the University of Texas System's founders. *Author's collection.*

UTMB, in 1965, released a master plan that showed the historic building being slated for demolition, and so it sat, deteriorating and waiting for the wrecking ball. As it waited, the once-grand east wing, which housed the original anatomy amphitheater, became a roost for pigeons. Then, in 1983, alumni and faculty from UTMB collaborated with the Galveston Historical Foundation to save the structure. The restoration of Old Red was completed three years later.

Medical Laboratory Building/Keiller Building
901–927 Strand Street

Designed in 1924 by the Dallas architect Herbert M. Greene and his eventual partner, George L. Dahl, this medical laboratory building corresponded to the university's main campus in Austin during the 1920s, primarily the 1918 Sutton Hall, designed by New York architect Cass Gilbert. The additions to campus in the 1930s were mostly the work of Robert Leon White, the university's consulting architect based out of Austin. A university-wide campaign by UTMB in the 1970s and 1980s resulted in the demolition of most of White's buildings, leaving Green's medical lab building behind.

Maison Rouge Ruins
1417 Harborside Drive

Not much remains of this old home, constructed in 1870: only a few stairs, some walls and portions of the floor and foundation. However, this site has ties to the days of piracy. Back in 1817, the notorious pirate—or privateer, as he preferred—Jean Lafitte settled on Galveston Island, with his ships and buccaneers, under the Mexican flag. From the island, they continued their forays out into the Gulf of Mexico against Spanish shipping galleons. At one point, Lafitte's force may have had as many as one thousand people, known as Baratarians, working for him. While he received a full pardon for his crimes due to assisting the Americans in defeating the British during the War of 1812, he soon turned back to smuggling.

While there are locales throughout the island associated with Lafitte and his pirates, he chose this spot to build his home, Maison Rouge—or Red House—in what was then Spanish Texas. His home was constructed to serve as part of his fort, and its upper story had designated spots for

While the ruins you see here are not those of Maison Rouge but of a home constructed in 1870, this was the site of pirate Jean Lafitte's home Maison Rouge from 1817 to 1821. His home was part of his fortress, and he even pierced the upper story of the building, placing a cannon inside the cavity to use as protection Inside, the home was furnished with items captured from ships. When Lafitte left the island, he burned it all. *Author's collection.*

cannon, while the interior was lavishly furnished with the spoils from captured ships. When Lafitte left Galveston in 1821, at the demand of the United States, he burned Maison Rouge, the fort and Campeche, the whole pirate village, then sailed to Yucatan. In 1870, the location became the site for a new home, constructed for a sea captain supposedly by the name of Hendricks and named Twelve Gables. The ruins you see today are of that more recent home.

Jack Johnson Childhood Homesite
808 Broadway

Few sites in Galveston remain from the life of boxing legend John Arthur "Jack" Johnson. Jack was born on the island on March 31, 1878, when Galveston was the largest city in the state. By the time he turned twenty-five, he had won the Negro Heavyweight Championship from Edward "Denver Ed" Martin, and he beat Tommy Burns in 1908, beginning a

The "Galveston Giant," Jack Johnson, was born on the island in 1878. He would eventually leave the island but returned for his boxing debut in 1898, winning the Texas State Middleweight Title. He would become the first African American heavyweight champion, fighting professionally until 1928. *Courtesy of the Ted Hood Portrait Collection, State Library of New South Wales.*

seven-year run as the undisputed heavyweight champion of the world. For years, racial discrimination kept him from his title shot, but by 1908, he was the only deserving contender, and he easily knocked out Burns for the belt.

Jack was the second child, and first son, of Henry and Tina Johnson's six children. The family were living on this site by the early 1880s, in a one-story wooden house, basement and enclosed porch that Henry Johnson himself built. Bullied as a young child, he took up boxing to protect himself and got good enough at the sport to beat everyone he could box on the island before moving to Chicago, home to some of the best boxers of the time. The Johnson home was destroyed during the 1900 Storm. This house replaced it in 1903.

In 1913, Johnson was convicted of violating the Mann Act of 1910, which made it a felony to engage in the "interstate commerce," or transport, of "any woman or girl for the purpose of prostitution or debauchery, or any other immoral purpose." While the law's stated purpose was to prevent human trafficking, it was also used to prosecute premarital, extramarital and interracial relationships. Johnson decided instead to skip bail and leave the country for the next seven years. When he returned to the States in 1920, he ended up serving ten months at the federal penitentiary at Fort Leavenworth. His other feats include a patent for a special kind of wrench and making his operatic debut in *Aida* in 1936. Johnson died from injuries sustained during an automobile accident in June 1946, near Raleigh, North Carolina.

Powhatan and Mattie Wren House
1403 Broadway

A side-gabled cottage, featuring galleries running the length of the north and south sides of the house, was constructed in 1873 for Edward Sylvester by W.C. Crookshank. It originally featured a small building at the back of the lot, which was used as a kitchen. Sylvester and his wife lived in the house for several years before selling to Powhatan and Mattie Wren. Powhatan S. Wren, a freight agent and later a city clerk, county clerk and chief clerk of the U.S. Customs House, hired contractor R.B. Garnett to renovate and enlarge the home in 1885. The house has kept this appearance since then, despite the 1900 Storm and the raising of the house afterward. The house remained in the family until 1921, then went through a series of owners throughout the following years. It was altered and became a rental property in the 1930s, remaining so throughout much of its life. Variations of this house can be seen in multiple homes throughout the district.

Fox House
1704 Market Street

On November 13, 1885, Galveston's great fire began just north of this home, near the corner of Sixteenth Street and Strand. With winds coming strong out of the north, the fire swept south and cut an enormous swath through this part of the East End before jumping Broadway to continue south toward Avenue O. As a result, the entire west side of the district was rebuilt in the 1880s, including this home. Nicholas Clayton altered and expanded a home moved onto this site for Christopher Fox, the Irish-American banking company owner. Much like the Runge House, this house faces the side street and includes a deep-set lawn on the south.

Jackson Building
1801–1803 Postoffice Street

Standing like a behemoth in a residential neighborhood, this two-story stucco and brick building served as one of the few corner stores in this affluent neighborhood. Typically, in these neighborhoods, this type of building would have been downsized in order to match the neighborhood massing. Despite this, from the moment it was conceptualized, the Jackson Building was actually used primarily as a boardinghouse. It was built for out-of-town investor James Jackson in 1887 as a replacement for a building destroyed in the fire. From the 1920s through the 1950s, the Jackson Building served as the playhouse of the Little Theater of Galveston. Most recently, it has served as the First Latin Assembly of God Church.

League House
1710 Broadway

This was the last grand house of Nicholas J. Clayton's work located in the Broadway Castle District, constructed in 1893 for real estate investor

John Charles League and his wife, daughter of George Ball. The property runs from Broadway all the way to Sealy Avenue, unusual at the time, but Clayton refrained from placing the front of the house facing its rear garden and instead chose to orient the house toward the street front on Broadway. One high-level feature of the property is the porte-cochere on the east side of the house.

From 1919 to 1947, the home was occupied by the matriarch of the Kempner family, Eliza Seinsheimer Kempner, widow of H. Kempner. Houston architect Birdsall Briscoe added a garden room to the back of the house and, in 1920, enclosed an open porch on the second floor's curved bay.

Chapter 5

SILK STOCKINGS DISTRICT

Galveston's Silk Stockings District is so named in reference to the early residents of the district. They were considered so wealthy that they could afford to buy silk stockings without a care. Originally, the suburb was developed in the early 1870s. Found in the district was a healthy mix of single-family homes, a small corner store, industrial sites and vacant blocks. The core of the district, however, until the 1890s, was the Texas Cotton Press. Following the press's bankruptcy and demolition, the area was subdivided, with the lots being sold at auction in 1898. Many of the homes built in this district survived the 1900 Storm and subsequent grade raising, when the seawall was built.

This neighborhood is the most intact residential area in the city from the late nineteenth and early twentieth centuries. Roughly bounded by Twenty-Fifth Street on the west and Twenty-Third Street on the east, with Avenue P on the south and Avenue K at the north, the district sports an impressive collection of homes dating from the Civil War through World War II and includes some of the island's notable Queen Anne architecture. The district was officially formed in April 1975 and was listed in the National Register of Historic Places in May 1996.

The Barber's Victorian Cottage
1314 Twenty-Fourth Street

This L-plan Victorian cottage, constructed in 1894 by island barber Adolph Helmann, survived the Storm of 1900. At this point in his career, Helmann was married to another second-generation German immigrant, Augusta Cassel, and had two children, Hazel and Naomi. He worked for P. Seidensticker, but within two years, he would own his own barbershop, located at 2008 Market Street. The family lived here at the time of the Hurricane. Hellman went on to take over the barbershop at the Tremont Hotel and ran that operation until his death in 1921. His widow sold this house the following September to James Maurer, one of Galveston's most prominent photographers. Maurer used the house as a tenant house before selling it in 1927 to Agnes Chapman, herself a widow with two young children. At the time of her husband's death, the Chapmans owned Galveston's famed Bettison Fishing Pier.

Smith Apartments
1103 Tremont Street

This 1903 boardinghouse was designed by Mrs. George C. Smith for her and her husband, George C., who was a Postal Telegraph-Cable Company telegraph operator. Standing at three stories, this was one of numerous apartment buildings built on the island in the early 1910s on prestigious Tremont Street. Equipped inside, for renters, were amenities such as ice-water dispensers, electrical call bells and speaking tubes. The apartment complex was rehabilitated in 1996.

Heiman Cottages
2318–2326 Avenue M

Meat Market proprietor Anton Heiman purchased two of the three lots here sometime around 1858 and had followed up that purchase with a third lot by 1861. By the end of the Civil War, these structures began popping up, all three examples of the Gulf Coast cottage despite their varying appearances. Additions to these structures—by then already described as "old" in insurance records—came about in less than a decade, as did a slight movement of the homes. The three homes were joined by a similar fourth home, located on the corner, and were shuffled closer together to make that happen.

Harris House
1303 Twenty-Fourth Street

This home was constructed in 1898 for sisters Frances, Bertha and Rosella Harris. This was one of the earliest homes constructed along Twenty-Fourth Street, and it sits within the heart of the Silk Stockings District. Like the other homes in the district, this one is aligned along the east and west sides of the streets, unlike Galveston's typical north and south orientations. Larger homes, such as this one, were built on the west side of Twenty-Fourth Street, so that the major rooms faced the prevailing gulf breeze. Additionally, denoting the divide of the streets, there is a continuous sidewalk on this side of the street, whereas the east side features a more intermittent sidewalk.

The Ball House
1405 Twenty-Fourth Street

When originally constructed, around 1854, this home was located on Tremont Street. It ended up on Twenty-Fourth Street, a victim of relocation, to make room for the construction of the Rosenberg Library in 1902. Constructed in the Greek Revival style for wholesale merchant George Ball, this home ended up with a touch of influence from famed Galveston architect Nicholas Clayton when he was hired for an improvement project in 1882, by homeowner Joseph G. Goldthwaite. When the home was purchased in 1902 by the wholesale grocer, importer and commission merchant John Focke, he was the one who moved it to its current site and, in the process, removed the rear wing, detaching and converting it into its own separate house. It is located next door at 1401 Twenty-Fourth Street.

Morrissey House
1508 Tremont Street

As it continues to be to this day, Broadway was Galveston's most fashionable residential streets in at the beginning of the twentieth century. Giving

Broadway a close run for its money was the tony Tremont Street. During the last twenty-five years of the twentieth century, homes such as the 1897 Morrissey House started cropping up. This two-story wood home was constructed for Martin P. Morrissey, the manager of a company that served as a steamship agent and imported building materials.

Hitchcock House
2209 Avenue K

Despite a long and storied history on the island, surviving numerous hurricanes and fires, this house has stood the test of time. It was moved to this location in 1996; however, it dates to much earlier. Records suggest that construction began before the Civil War for at least some sections of the home. It was originally located at Twenty-First Street and Avenue K and belonged to L.M. Hitchcock Jr., who had owned the property since 1839.

Saint Joseph's Catholic Church
2202 Avenue K

Originally, when constructed by Joseph Bleicke in 1859, this wood church served Galveston's German parish, St. Joseph's. It stands as the oldest wooden church building on the island; however, it was virtually destroyed during the 1900 Storm. Under architect Nicholas Clayton's direction, the church was rebuilt. Clayton added a new sanctuary, and his sacristies flank the rear of the church. The ornate interior belies the rather plain exterior; also inside are the original cedar pews, hand-carved altars and plaster stations of the cross. The Galveston Historical Foundation took over the building's maintenance as a historical site, and it is open by special arrangement.

Chapter 6

LOST BAYOU DISTRICT

The Lost Bayou District is the island's newest designated local historic district. It originally received this designation in 1994; that later expanded to include an additional, but noncontiguous, block in 2004. It covers roughly twenty-three blocks on the south side of Broadway Boulevard and between Twenty-First and Sixteenth Streets, and its name, Lost Bayou, refers back to Hitchcock's Bayou, which became lost during the aftermath of the 1900 Storm. The bayou was filled in when the seawall was constructed and the island's grade was raised behind it.

For the longest time, much of the area between the Gulf of Mexico and Avenue L, and between Twentieth and Twenty-Third Streets, was covered by Hitchcock's Bayou. The bayou was even the preferred water source for the military camels that were residing on the island in the 1850s. Their corral was situated directly behind where the Brian Museum currently sits. Prior to the 1900 Storm, the area east of the bayou suffered greatly during the great fire of 1885. It started near Sixteenth and Strand and extended all the way to the Gulf of Mexico, eating many of the homes and structures adjacent to the bayou.

Originally, this neighborhood developed around the same time as the East End and Silk Stockings Historic District—although on a smaller scale than the others. Today, it includes numerous twentieth-century homes, many built following the 1900 Storm, which ravaged the area. Also, like its East End neighbors, it is laid out on a grid system, with most homes facing east–west avenues and but a few on each block facing the north–south streets.

Charles Albertson, cotton buyer, built his house in 1870 in the Lost Bayou section of the San Jacinto Historical District. It was severely damaged during the 1900 Storm but still stood. The house was purchased, remodeled and moved slightly after Ben Blum bought it in 1903. *Author's collection.*

Lindenberg Home
2116 Avenue K

This home once served as the home of Professor Emil Lindenberg. Alfred Muller designed it in 1887 for Lindenberg, who was Galveston's foremost bandleader during the 1880s and 1890s. If you look closely, the home's porch gable design still features the identifying mark of Lindenberg's island fame: a lyre, denoting the homeowner's notoriety.

The Carroll House
1717 Avenue K

When you need a home, you need a home. Unfortunately for pilot Rucker T. Carroll, his timing could not have been worse. His new two-story side-hall house was constructed in August 1900. Presciently, he had it built on brick piers that were seven and a half feet tall. Despite this, the storm the following month took that house right off its foundation. Fortunately for Carroll, the house was not destroyed. While nearly all of Galveston's buildings sustained some form of damage during the hurricane, many of those were able to withstand the storm relatively intact. Likely, Pilot Carroll's home managed to survive as one of the latter.

Engine House No. 5
1614 Avenue K

While the construction style of fire engine houses of the nineteenth century generally does not align with neighborhood residential architectural styles, this firehouse does align closely in scale and detail. Standing at two stories, with a stucco face atop brick architecture, this firehouse was constructed in 1891 by W.H. Tyndall, one of several that he designed on the island but the only one still left standing. It was constructed on its site, flush with its sidewalk, much as if it was placed in a more commercial part of town.

Lasker Home for Homeless Children
1017 Sixteenth Street

Originally, this home served as the family home of Marcus C. McLemore, a prominent Galveston lawyer. McLemore had purchased two lots in 1868, and during the following couple of years, he had this imposing galleried house constructed. In 1901, the Society for the Help of Homeless Children purchased the house and property for organizational purposes and converted the home into an orphanage.

Victorian Row Houses
1424–1428 Avenue K

These three sister houses were constructed around 1895, possibly by Alfred Muller. Decorative panels of shingles located beneath the windows on the side of the home at 1424 Avenue K are indicative of Muller's work. At three bays wide and standing at two stories, these Victorian southern townhomes are great examples of Galveston's nineteenth-century architecture prior to the 1900 Storm.

Galveston Orphans Home
1313 Twenty-First Street

The block surrounding the Twenty-First Street and Avenue M corner was, prior to 1873, the site of Hitchcock's Bayou. This was one of two draws, filled with salt water, that coursed through the southern half of the island prior to emptying out into the gulf. As the city grew, the bayou was dammed, drained and filled in by the city. This afforded developers new neighborhood space south of Avenue L for development. Those plots along Twenty-First Street were extremely attractive, for they ran along the tracks of Galveston's horsecar system from the city to the beach.

This large, grandiose building on Twenty-First Street was designed by George B. Stowe and erected in 1902. This version of the George Dealy–founded Galveston Orphans Home, also known as the Galveston Children's Home, was constructed to replace Alfred Muller's original design from 1895. That version, constructed by local builder Harry Devlin

When a new Galveston Orphans Home opened in 1895 to replace the Island City Orphans Home, it only lasted a short while. It was heavily damaged during the 1900 Storm. A charity bazaar, sponsored by William Randolph Hearst, was held to raise funds to rebuild. This new iteration was dedicated in 1902 and operated until 1984, when it was consolidated with other island programs. The Bryan Museum, which opened in 2015, is housed here today. *Author's collection.*

in the Renaissance Revival style, was so severely damaged during the 1900 Storm that demolition was the only recourse.

Standing by itself on a full block, the Galveston Orphans Home, with its stately live oaks, quickly achieved a southern likeness resembling homes in New Orleans's Garden District. The brown brick building, with its cement plaster–surfaced walls, itself came from the philanthropic pocketbook of William Randolph Hearst, through a charity bazaar in New York City, and that of local philanthropist Henry Rosenberg.

Following the building's use as a home for orphans for nearly a century, Galveston's multiple orphanages combined to create the Children's Center Inc. After the Children's Center moved to a different location, this building sat vacant until it was rehabilitated as a private residence. In October 2013, J.P. and Mary Jon Bryan purchased the building. Following a careful and extensive restoration, it opened as the Bryan Museum in June 2015 and features twenty thousand square feet of space for exhibits related to Texas history.

Franklin-Wandless House
1920 Avenue M

The Franklin-Wandless House was constructed in 1886, replacing a home destroyed in the great Strand fire. It was home to Robert Morris and Sarah Franklin. Most likely designed by Galveston architect Nathaniel Tobey, who also designed the Galveston Opera House, it survived the 1900 Storm with three feet of water in the downstairs rooms. In the storm's aftermath, Franklin played an active part in planning the seawall. John Wandless, a veteran of the Boer War and World War I and a former journalist, came to Galveston in 1921. He and his wife, Vera, bought the house from the Franklin heirs in 1931.

The Franklin-Wandless House was built in 1886 to replace a house destroyed in the Strand fire. It was likely designed by Nathaniel Tobey, whose other works include the Galveston Opera House. The home survived the 1900 Storm with three feet of water inside. Robert Franklin, the original owner, was actively involved in the planning of the seawall. *Author's collection.*

Muller Home
2111 Avenue M½

Famed Galveston architect Alfred Muller and his family were living in this small rental home—located directly across the street from what might have been his most grand project on the island—at the time of his death of typhoid fever in 1896. Muller did not design this home; instead, it was built by house painter Christian Walker, who lived relatively nearby in the 2800 block of Avenue L. This was not an uncommon practice. The small row of dwellings located here exemplifies one of several types of houses built during this time throughout the city by either contractors or builders, without the aid of a professional architect.

Coppersmith Inn Bed & Breakfast
1914 Avenue M

Constructed in 1887 by Alfred Muller, this two-story house is a complicated version of the southern townhouse style and contains an angled bay located on the west corner, which rises into an implied tower. Built for Howard Carnes, who was a cashier in the Galveston office of a regional steamship and railroad corporation, Muller's home is set along the ground. It's unlikely that the house was designed in this fashion; it is more likely the result of not altering the house when the grade raising came through and filled in the ground level of the house. Today, the home serves as the Coppersmith Inn B&B.

The Wharf Worker's Cottage
1212 Nineteenth Street

This one-bedroom, one-bathroom cottage was originally used as a rental property for Galveston port and wharf employees. German immigrant Julius Lobenstein built the home five years after the great fire of 1885 from remains he gathered from other burned structures, attempting to utilize as many of the materials surrounding him as possible. This led to a mismatch of wood and paint colors, as all the walls and ceilings came from houses built between 1860 and 1885. The house remained in the Lobenstein family until 1943.

Chapter 7

CEDAR LAWN HISTORIC DISTRICT

The Cedar Lawn neighborhood, established in 1926, was Galveston's first fully planned residential community. This ambitious development was instigated by W.L. Moody III; his brother-in-law Clark W. Thompson, a dry goods merchant and future congressman; and W.D. Harden. Covering nine square blocks, the Cedar Lawn District is located just two blocks south of Broadway. These eclectic homes are situated in a butterfly pattern, which was unique in the southwestern United States at that time. The homes range from small dwellings to expansive mansions, many of them dominated by brick façades. This feature, along with the neighborhood's accompanying restrictions and rules, as well as the lack of commercial intrusion, has led this neighborhood to retain a high level of historic integrity. Cedar Lawn received its nomination for inclusion on the National Register of Historic Places in 2002 and became a local conservation district in 2017.

Sam Maceo House
43 Cedar Lawn Circle

This sprawling home was designed by Ross Patton of the firm Williams, Williams & Williams. Ross, a well-known Palm Desert architect during the 1950s–70s, also designed Frank Sinatra's Villa Maggio above the Coachella Valley. Maceo's casino and other business operations typically saw visitation from some of the biggest entertainers at the time, including Sinatra, whom

Maceo had visited while in Palm Springs. Sam Maceo had the house built in 1952, having become a successful organized crime boss who established Galveston island as a resort town, open to vices throughout. To finish the interior, Maceo and his wife, Edna Sedgwick, hired a decorator out of New York.

The seven-bedroom, ten-bath house sits on an acre and features a beautiful outdoor space that includes a pool and a "chauffeur's house" (or guest suite). The 6,300-square-foot house is laid out in an L-shaped pattern and is constructed of brick, timber, glass and stone. Maceo never got to live in the house; he died of cancer at the age of fifty-seven in 1951. His wife, Edna, a dancer and actor, with whom he had twin sons and one daughter, moved in but only for a short while. When the home came up for sale in 2017, the initial asking price was $1.15 million.

W.L. Moody III House
16 Cedar Lawn Drive South

Designed by Alfred C. Finn, in 1929, this house was built that same year by island businessman and philanthropist W.L. Moody III. Finn's residential designer, Robert Smallwood, provided Finn with a pedimented Georgian-style country house. It is one of the grandest homes on the island. Smallwood, in 1930, would add a swimming pool, bathhouse, tropical greenhouse and gardener's cottage, all of which back up to Cedar Lawn Circle. The house was acquired by Shearn Moody, W.L.'s brother.

The Loomis House
15 Cedar Lawn Circle

Designed by Michael A. Loomis in 1949, this was the first of his freewheeling Contemporary-style houses. It was built for his own family and has been lived in by members of the family since. Glass blocks and the curved polished red concrete front steps are what truly stand out about this home. An entrance pylon tower of red glazed brick greets you when you arrive at the house. Just down the road, located at 26 Cedar Lawn Circle, sits Loranzy Grillete's house. Loranzy was Sam Maceo's lieutenant. His house was constructed in 1951, also by Michael Loomis.

Chapter 8

OUT WEST

Galveston's San Jacinto neighborhood has one of the longest stretches of beach frontage on the island. Historically, it was the San Jacinto neighborhood that served as the heart of the island's tourist industry and beach development. This historic neighborhood covers an area of more than 150 square blocks on the east end of the island. Forming a rough triangle, the district is bounded by the Seawall Boulevard, Broadway and Twenty-Third Street, and within those boundaries also lies the Lost Bayou Historic District. When it received its historic designation, it was the first conservation district in Galveston, one of only a few in Texas (none of which were located in Houston).

The neighborhood today includes modest homes from the late nineteenth and early twentieth centuries, with a few of the grander structures littered throughout the region. While there is an eclectic mix of architectural styles, the more dominant styles you will find are Greek Revival, Arts and Crafts, Folk Victorian and Italianate. Unfortunately, the San Jacinto neighborhood bore the brunt of the 1900 Hurricane. Indeed, the neighborhood may have stretched four blocks farther into the Gulf of Mexico than it does presently. Those buildings closest to the beach suffered the worst; debris from the homes actually formed a breakwater, thus helping to save the rest of the island from the same fate.

SAN JACINTO NEIGHBORHOOD

Graugnard's Bakery Building
1227 Avenue L

Sitting empty and for sale as recently as 2023, the Graugnard's Building is a streamlined modernistic-style baking plant. Located on the street corner, the plant extends from the corner both south and west. Projecting hoods set above the second-story windows are repeated at the front opening of the building as well.

Williams Manor
4505 Caduceus Place

Designed by San Antonio architects Phelps and Dewees for lawyer Brian F. Williams, this home sits at the entrance to Galveston's prestigious and restricted two-block neighborhood called Caduceus Place. Like the others in the enclave, this buff brick–faced home was designed to be insulated from those homes located in the Groesbeck grid by having a private street located along the alley line. Other distinctions unique to the neighborhood are the rose-colored concrete roads and the brick and cast stone gate piers at Forty-Fifth Street.

Moody House
5115 Avenue T

This stands as one of John F. Staub's largest Galveston homes. The home, constructed in 1938, even features a driveway with its own street sign. The home, designed to be a country house set on a small estate, is set back from the neighbors and streets by walls and vegetation. It was built for W.L. Moody III and his wife, Mary Margaret Guinard. Moody had built the largest home in the neighborhood, just as he did in the Cedar Lawn neighborhood back in the 1920s.

Lakeview Cemetery
3015 Fifty-Seventh Street

Set off from the massive stretch of cemeteries along Broadway Avenue, Lakeview Cemetery seems almost like an afterthought. On top of that, the maintenance at the cemetery isn't always the most consistent, leaving it prone to overgrowth. The positive about that is one gets to see a part of the island unfettered by too much progress.

Standing guard over the tombs is the Galveston Tidal Wave Monument. Designed and sculpted by Pompeo Coppini in 1905, it was erected by the Woodmen of the World (WoW), the fraternal organization and insurance company based out of Omaha, Nebraska. Featured here is the bronze figure of Joseph C. Root, the Iowa businessman who founded WoW. It stands as a memorial to WoW members who died during the 1900 Storm.

Robert's Lafitte
2501 Avenue Q

Established in 1965, Robert's Lafitte is Texas's oldest gay bar. Calton LeBlanc opened the bar first at 305 Rosenberg, a location that is today an empty lot. Robert Mainor purchased the club in 1970 and, after a fire destroyed the original location, moved it first to Twenty-Second and Strand before finally settling here. Named for the famed pirate and smuggler Jean Lafitte, it is renowned for its drag shows on the weekends. Following Hurricane Ike in 2008, it was one of the first establishments on the to get island up and running again. The two-story commercial building was constructed about 1920 and has been altered for various uses since.

Van Alstyne House
2901 Broadway

Many places claim to be the most haunted location on Galveston Island. Known as Broadway's "Gingerbread House," the Van Alstyne House was constructed in 1891. Standing three stories tall, this Victorian mansion stretches out across 6,300 square feet, contains fourteen rooms and was commissioned by Alfred Albert and his wife, Catherine. A few short years later, the great storm of 1900 struck the island. As the wind whipped down

Located on Avenue Q, Robert's Lafitte is the oldest gay bar in Texas. Calton LeBlanc opened it in 1965 as Lafitte's, named for the famed smuggler and pirate. When Robert Mainor bought it in 1970, he changed the moniker to its present name to distinguish it from New Orleans' Cafe Lafitte in Exile, the oldest continually operating gay bar in the United States. *Author's collection.*

the streets and rain pelted everyone on the street, Catherine opened her doors to fifty Galvestonians, huddling with them under the staircase of the house. The Van Alstyne house managed to survive while much of the surrounding neighborhood was devastated. Albert died within the walls of the Van Alstyne House in 1926, and his beloved Catherine followed in 1940. The home later became Antebellum Antiques; stories of paranormal activity have abounded since those early days.

Ursuline Convent and Academy Site
2601 Avenue M

Galveston's Ursuline Academy was established in February 1847 by the Ursuline Sisters from New Orleans. They established the island's first parochial school, opening its doors on a ten-acre campus in 1854. It closed for only a short time in 1857, during a yellow fever epidemic, managing to stay open during the Civil War while being used as a hospital by both sides. Then, during the 1900 Storm, the main Victorian Gothic building, which was constructed by Nicholas Clayton with the convent in the mid-1890s, sheltered more than one thousand refugees. In January 1947, the school celebrated its centennial. The campus contained the academy building, a brick chapel and a monastery situated on roughly eight acres. When Hurricane Carla struck Galveston in 1961, both the academy and the convent sustained damage and were subsequently demolished. The chapel stood from 1871 to 1961 and the convent from 1854 to 1973. In 1968, the girls' school consolidated with the island's Dominican girls' school and Kirwin Catholic High School; it was renamed O'Connell High School.

African American Museum
3427 Sealy

This smaller museum is located in a house near Galveston ISD's Central Media Arts Academy. Don't worry, this bright green two-story house will be easy to find. The exterior walls feature portraits of prominent African American Galvestonians painted by local artist E. Herron. The museum opened in 2003 under the leadership and efforts of James Josey, who grew up on the island. Some of those featured include Galveston's first Black female police officer,

Decorated with numerous images and stories of island trailblazers on its facade, the Galveston African American Museum highlights those African Americans who have made significant contributions to the community. If you are looking to delve further into these cultural sites of the island's history, this is a great place to get a start. *Author's collection.*

Annie Mae Charles; Jack Johnson, who became the first Black heavyweight boxing champion; and R&B great Barry White, and Dr. Beverly Lewis, the University of Texas Medical Branch's first Black female surgeon.

Yeager's Children Home
1111 Thirty-Second Street

The Yeager Children's Home was founded in 1917 by Albertine Hall Yeager, an African American woman. Yeager opened her business during the era of Jim Crow laws, increasing segregation throughout Texas. Her aim to help Black families by opening an orphanage and day care center was ambitious. However, with desegregation merely on a horizon ten years ahead and the Ku Klux Klan holding open rallies on East Beach, she expanded her business to assisting White families as well.

Along with her husband, Charlie, Yeager founded the home shortly after moving to the island from Palestine, Texas. At that time, there were only six private orphanages in the state for Black children. The day care center opened as a resource for mothers working in war industries during the First World War. During World War II, she expanded the business to care for children regardless of race or religion. According to her obituary, Yeager likely provided care to one thousand children during her life.

The historic marker was produced by the Texas Historical Commission, via their Untold Marker program. It honors Yeager and was erected in 2022, on the orphanage's original location. The original Yeager Children's Home was demolished in 1974 and replaced with a newer structure run by the Children's Center, which continues to operate a shelter for families and young people. This newer organization is developing a portion of the site as the Albertine Hall Yeager Youth Cultural Center, complete with a historic display and education center.

THE WEST END

Avenue L Missionary Baptist Church
2612 Avenue L

Avenue L Missionary Baptist Church stands as one of the oldest Black congregations in Texas. Organized in 1840 by Reverend James Huckins, this church grew out of the slave membership from the First Baptist Church of Galveston, who had begun worshipping in a separate building by the 1850s. By this point, they were known as the African Baptist Church. First Baptist trustees James Huckins, John S. Sydnor and Gail Borden Jr. purchased land for the fellowship in 1855, and following the Civil War, the property was formally deeded to the congregation, where it was reorganized as the First Regular Missionary Baptist Church. The 1900 Storm destroyed the congregation's original building. Following the storm, a wood replacement church building was constructed and utilized until the Tanner Brothers Contractors and Architects, an African American firm, constructed the replacement building in 1916, which stands there to this day. Visible on the west side of the brick church is the wooden church building from 1904.

Central High School/Old Central Cultural Center
2627 Avenue M

The first African American high school in the state of Texas was established in Galveston in 1885. In 1893, Nicholas Clayton designed a permanent two-story brick building to be used as a free public school for African American students in Galveston. In 1904, the growing student population necessitated an enlargement to the building, and an annex to the school was constructed to be used as the school's library. Before this school closed, by the time Galveston's schools were integrated in 1968, thousands of Galveston's African American students had passed through these halls. By the time the school was shuttered, it was located at its fourth site, a building currently being used as Galveston's middle school. This building, the school's third location, was saved in large part due to the establishment of the Old Central Cultural Center Inc. in 1974. The preservation and operation of the building and site of the first public school and library for African Americans in the state has been under their purview since. It is being maintained to provide Galveston with a community center, provide programs and cultural enrichment and preserve Galveston's African American history and heritage.

Jack Johnson Park
2601 Avenue M

Born on the island on March 31, 1878, John Arthur "Jack" Johnson is one of Galveston's biggest names. In 1903, he won the Negro Heavyweight Championship, and in 1908, he beat Tommy Burns to become the undisputed heavyweight champion of the world. He held onto the title for the next seven years. This park, dedicated on November 13, 2012, features a life-size bronze statue of the "Galveston Giant" and is adjacent to the Old Central Cultural Center.

Grace Episcopal Church
1115 Thirty-Sixth Street

Formed initially as a mission Sunday school founded by the Rectory of Trinity Church on the island, this church was located here for the convenience of the outlying areas of Galveston in the 1840s. Members of the congregation received permission in 1876 from the rector to establish Grace Episcopal Church. Their first sanctuary was in a wooden building, then located at the corner of Avenue L and Thirty-Sixth Street. Island benefactor Henry Rosenberg gifted the church a large sum for a new building. Nicholas Clayton's expertise with houses of worship was called on, and he designed a High Victorian Gothic stone church building as a result. The old building was moved down the street, and the new building was completed in 1895. The church survived the 1900 Storm and served as a place of refuge for many. That original wooden church, which had been moved behind the new stone church, was completely washed away, however. Following the storm, the church was raised four and a half feet. Over the years, the congregation has ebbed and flowed, and the church has moved in and out of its mission status.

Eiband House
3112 Broadway

Architect Raymond Rapp designed this brick Colonial Revival house for Joseph and Judith Eiband in 1928. Joseph was then working as the general manager of Eiband's Department Store downtown. That operation had been founded by his father in 1895. At one point, Eiband's was the largest privately owned retailer in the United States. This home stands as one of the last residences constructed for a prominent Galveston family on the grand boulevard of Broadway. Around this time, Broadway was declared a state highway and became the first paved roadway to Houston.

BROADWAY CEMETERY HISTORIC DISTRICT

Occupying six city blocks, this land was originally set aside for family burial purposes as part of the original town charter in 1839. The cemeteries sport a wide variety of monuments, from simple marble and granite markers to large Classical Revival vaults, mausoleums in the Gothic Revival style and tall obelisks peeking above. As beliefs and traditions changed, or were enhanced, burial practices changed with them and now provide a vast landscape of cultural and historical significance. This urban cemetery remains as a rare example of its type within the state, as many were abandoned during the nineteenth century. The burial grounds here are seven cemeteries, many of

Covering six city blocks, the Broadway Cemeteries complex is composed of seven separate cemeteries. Originally, the land was set aside in the town charter for family burial purposes in 1839. It is a rare surviving example of this type of urban cemetery within Texas. Visit in the spring and you'll get a chance to see the amazing flowers that spread throughout the grounds. *Author's collection.*

them in response to nine devastating yellow fever epidemics from 1839 to 1867. Nearly 60 percent of Galveston's population was affected by multiple yellow fever epidemics in 1853, resulting in a death toll of 523; in 1867, hundreds more died.

The cemeteries in this district are Old City Cemetery (1839); Oleander Cemetery (1839), which was originally known as Potter's Field; Evergreen Cemetery (1839); Old Catholic Cemetery (ca. 1844); Episcopal Cemetery (1844); Hebrew Benevolent Society Cemetery (1868); and New City Cemetery (1900), which was established in response to the 1900 Storm. Names like Hitchcock, Turehears, Childress, Magruder, Menard, Williams and Cherry can all be found here, among so many other prominent Galveston names. The cemeteries have been raised a few times in different areas; many times, stones were lost in these raisings, leading to the reselling of plots with another burial on top of the previous one. The last raising came in the 1920s. An estimated twelve thousand grave markers remain visible in the cemeteries—representing roughly only a quarter of those buried here.

Kempner Park
2704 Avenue O

In February 1876, a group of German businessmen purchased a five-acre plot of land to be used as a social club for their family and friends. The Galveston Garten Verein, or Garden Club, included a clubhouse, lawns, walkways, tennis courts, playgrounds, croquet grounds, bowling alleys, a bandstand and a dancing pavilion. Dances, parties, picnics and concerts were frequently held at the park during the spring and summer months.

The dancing pavilion, still standing, was completed in 1880 with a party thrown for President Ulysses S. Grant and General Phil Sheridan, who had stopped in Galveston on their way home from a vacation in Mexico. The long-lived popularity of the park and its facilities came to a screeching halt during and after World War I, however. Anti-German sentiment bled into every part of the country. In 1923, members of the club voted to sell the property as a result. Stanley E. Kempner, a Galveston insurance executive, purchased the property and, in turn, donated it to the city as a public park dedicated to his own parents, Harris and Eliza Kempner.

Kempner Park has long been a staple of recreational life on the island. The dancing pavilion is now known as the Garten Verein Pavilion; the Albert Kuhn Memorial Pergola, which was built in 1911, continues to stand

The Garten Verein Pavilion is in Kempner Park on Avenue O. It remains one of Galveston's most popular special event venues. The historic tiered dancing pavilion is housed in a unique octagonal design with panoramic windows for views at all angles. It is one of the few structures to survive the 1900 Storm. *Author's collection.*

as well—despite the destruction of two major storms and a fire. The 1900 Storm left debris piled up throughout the park, in places five to ten feet high. When Ike came ashore in 2008, it also caused notable damage to the pavilion and the landscaping. Again, they were restored to prominence, and the park is just as beautiful and as accessible as ever.

John H. Hutchings House
2816 Avenue O

John Henry Hutchins and his wife, Minni, had this home—designed to resemble an Italian villa—built in 1856. Hutchins was notable in town for his work with George Bell and John Sealy dealing in banking and commissions. The home, constructed on five acres that came to the Hutchins family as a wedding gift from Minni's uncle Robert Mills, was one of Galveston's rare early brick homes, fired on Mills's Brazoria plantation. The house included a half-story schoolroom and teacher's quarters.

Following damage from an 1885 storm, architect Nicholas Clayton was hired to do an extensive repair and renovation job on the home. Because of this, the home has become a mixture of the Romanesque and Renaissance Revival styles. Clayton removed the south gallery, with its single-story porch, and the west porch, which featured a two-story gabled portico, but added a third floor and applied stucco to the house's brick walls. He also constructed the carriage house and completed other renovations by 1889. The home was raised following the 1900 Storm and remained in the family until 1926 before returning to the family again in 1946. It became a Recorded Texas Historic Landmark in 1962.

Galveston Artillery Club
3102 Avenue O

While this building is relatively new, constructed in the 1950s, its origins date to the Republic. On September 13, 1840, a group of local businessmen, and their clerks, banded together to organize the Galveston Artillery Company. At that time, the city hosted roughly 1,200 residents, served as the entry point for numerous immigrants and was a major coastal shipping port. That, coupled with ongoing tensions between the new republic and neighboring Mexico, led to the establishment of several volunteer militia groups, including the Galveston Artillery Company, which received charters to protect the harbor and the city.

In reality, what the company did was mostly perfunctory acts: participating in parades, drills, commemorations and musters and hosting lavish balls. They were rarely called into state service; however, they did participate in calling for the Federal surrender of Fort Brown in traveling with other companies to Brownsville at the outbreak of the Civil War. During the war, the company disbanded, as its members had been spread throughout the country due to the conflict. Following the war, the company underwent several reorganizations. By 1899, it had become the Galveston Artillery Club, more a social organization than a military one, which it is to this day. The company met at various locations throughout the city before its new clubhouse, designed by Thomas M. Price, was completed in 1959.

Michel Menard House
1605 Thirty-Third Street

Known also as the Oaks, the Menard House is the oldest surviving structure in Galveston, having been constructed in 1838. Named for Canadian-born trader and real estate investor Michel Branamour Menard, this home was outside of Galveston's city limits when it was constructed. Menard had worked with John Jacob Astor's fur trading company at the age of fourteen. When he arrived in Nacogdoches in the 1830s, he immediately began speculating in land, much of which was surveyed by Juan Seguin, who purchased land on the island on Menard's behalf.

Michel B. Menard was a British North American trader and merchant. He began his career on the upper Mississippi River before moving south to Texas, where he established a fur-trading post at Nacogdoches before moving to Galveston Island. With acreage owned on the island from work with Juan Seguin, he established and founded the town of Galveston. *Courtesy of the Library of Congress.*

Menard, one of Galveston's city fathers, had his home fabricated and shipped from Maine in parts to Galveston for construction. He started construction on the home in 1837, building it for his second wife, Catherine Maxwell. John Kirby Allen would buy the home in July of 1838, then, in 1843, a cousin deeded the property to Menard's third wife, Mary Jane Riddle Menard. She lived in the house until her death that December. He would later marry Rebecca Mary Bass, adoped her two children, and then had one of their own as a couple. The growing family resulted in the addition of two wings to the home.

The home would serve, in 1853, as the site for Galveston's first Mardi Gras ball. Menard wouldn't spend much longer in the house, however. In 1856, he, too, passed away. Four years later, his widow, Rebecca, married Colonel J.S. Thrasher, the former U.S. consul at Havana. The home was sold by the Menard family in 1880 to Edwin Ketchum, whose family kept control of the home until 1977. In 1994, the deteriorating home began undergoing restoration and was finished in time for the 1995 Historic Homes Tour.

Mexican Telegraph Company Transmission Shack
1605 Thirty-Third Street

This small house, more a shack than anything else, once stood at 1819 Avenue O. Inside was telegraph equipment that relayed messages from throughout the world to Galveston and then on into Mexico. This was done via the Mexican Telegraph Company Trans-Gulf Cable, which entered Galveston beneath the seawall near Nineteenth Street.

In 1917, during World War I, German military leaders found the war at a stalemate. They adopted an aggressive strategy that involved striking any ships—even those from neutral nations—that were encountered in the Atlantic. In the hopes of hindering the United States entering the war, the German secretary for foreign affairs, Arthur Zimmerman, approved a message to Mexican president Venustiano Carranza. It was to offer Carranza financial support and other considerations if Mexico would invade the American Southwest.

The restored home of the Mexican Telegraph Company's Galveston transmission shack is now located on the property of Michel Menard's historic home. The Zimmerman Telegram, which played a prominent role in galvanizing support for the United States' involvement in World War I, was relayed through this structure in 1917. *Author's collection.*

Unfortunately for the Germans, they were unable to hand deliver such a message to Mexico's envoy, so instead, they decided to transmit the telegram from Germany to Washington, D.C., and in turn, the German ambassador would send it on to Mexico City via the German station in Galveston on Avenue O. The telegram was sent on January 16, 1917, and British intelligence agents, who were monitoring messages via the U.S. embassy in London, intercepted the message and were able to decipher it, giving U.S. officials a copy on February 19.

The message, on review, caused President Woodrow Wilson to abandon his hopes for a peaceful conclusion to the war and, in turn, arranged for a copy to be leaked to the press. The story helped accelerate the United States' entry into the war, which would eventually lead to victory for the allies. In the years following the 1918 Armistice, the Mexican Telegraph Company ultimately merged with Western Union, remaining open until 1949. It was located on the property of the Pompeo Urbani family, who ran a grocery store at Nineteenth Street and Avenue O for most of the twentieth century. This small building was a shed next to their store for years. In order to prevent its demolition, the historic shack was moved to its current location in the rear of the Menard House in 1995 and restored.

Powhatan House
3427 Avenue O

The Powhatan House was built as the home of Colonel John Seabrook Sydnor, prominent cotton merchant, slave dealer, financier and early Galveston mayor. The Greek Revival home is one of the oldest existing structures on the island. Colonel Sydnor—an early proponent of the importation of "cotton culture," already was established in the rest of the South, into Texas—migrated to Galveston from Virginia in 1838. When he witnessed what Galveston was becoming as a major port of entry for all of Texas trade and immigration, he quickly began investing in real estate and formed his own cotton merchant, the J.S. Sydnor & Co. cotton wholesalers, a leader in Galveston cotton wholesale business until 1866. By 1840, he had moved his entire family to the island and been elected to the city board of aldermen. His influence in Galveston was widespread. He hauled cotton from the plantations along the Brazos River to Galveston, had the "Brick Wharf" built on the island for cotton storage, initiated commercial exploitation of Galveston Bay's oyster bed, served as mayor,

During the 1850s, Galveston exported goods, primarily cotton, valued at almost twenty times what was imported. By 1878, the Port of Galveston was the nation's third-largest cotton exporter, but by 1882, it had fallen to fifth. While it was outpaced in the industrial exports, it remained a strong port for agricultural goods. This postcard shows the loading of cotton onto ships at the port. *Courtesy of University of Texas at Arlington Libraries.*

organized the chamber of commerce and fostered trade with other ports. He also promoted the railroad causeway to link the island with the mainland, helped organize the police and fire departments and opened the city's first free public school.

The Sydnors' home, constructed in 1847, was intended as a showplace for their wealth. The twenty-four-room Doric Greek Revival home was dubbed Powhatan after the tribes in Colonel Sydnor's native Virginia. The original home had a six-column portico and a raised basement, or ground floor. Five acres of gardens were on the grounds, featuring Galveston's famed oleanders. Like the nearby Menard House and the Samuel May Williams House, it was framed in a seaport in Maine and shipped to the island for construction. Sydnor tried to operate the house as a hotel for a while, but its distance from the wharves and downtown was too great, so he converted it back to a residence.

Sydnor remained in Galveston until the close of the Civil War. Following the war, in 1866, he dissolved his partnership in his own trading firm and moved to New York to act as a trading agent for Galveston cotton interests. Additionally, he liquidated most of his Galveston holdings, sold the Powhatan

House to a Mr. Bolton and did not return to Texas again until 1869, when he died while visiting his son. Later attempts to open the house as a school and miliary academy were unsuccessful. It operated as an orphanage and served as a consulate building for the British government before finally being purchased and restored in 1965 by the Galveston Garden Club.

Robert Hutchings House
1718 Thirty-Fifth Street

This small stucco home, constructed in 1934, was designed by Galveston-born architect Donald Barthelme to resemble a French manor. It is the only extant of Barthelme's creations left. Barthelme's fame is more closely linked to his work for the 1936 Texas Centennial Exposition in Dallas, for which he served as chief designer; from there, he went on to become a prominent architect in Houston. This home was designed while he was practicing on the island during the Great Depression, for Robert K. Hutchings and his wife, Drusilla Davis.

Miss Matilda Waters House
3518 Avenue O

This home, constructed in 1897 and raised, was built for Captain George Wilson. This area of town, west of Thirty-Fifth Street, showcases a late Victorian middle-class neighborhood. This home specifically was where Matilda Walters moved when she retired as the Line's noted madam, Mollie Waters.

Magnolia Petroleum Company Filling Station 134
3827 Avenue O

This is one of the oldest—if not *the* oldest—surviving gas stations in Galveston. Facing Thirty-Ninth Street, Filling Station 134 was constructed in 1926 for the Magnolia Petroleum Company. John Sealy organized the Magnolia Petroleum Company with his brother-in-law R. Waverly Smith, naming the company for his aunt, Magnolia Willis Sealy. The company would later become part of Mobil Oil Corporation.

Samuel May Williams House
3601 Avenue P

Samuel May Williams had this home shipped to him on a schooner following its framing in Maine. Williams was a founder of Galveston, secretary to Stephen F. Austin, postmaster and land agent of the Austin colony and organizer of the first bank in Texas and is considered the father of the Texas navy and its shipping industry. He had come to Austin's Texas colony in 1823, having likely met Austin sometime around 1819 in New Orleans. For his services in working with Austin and due to his immigrant status (Texas was not a state at the time), Williams was given eleven leagues.

In 1833, Williams founded a business with Thomas McKinney in Quintana, located at the mouth of the Brazos River. When Williams traveled into the States in 1835 in order to sell some bank stock, he learned of fighting breaking out in Texas. Using the partnership's credit, he began making purchases for the Texas army and supporting the Texas revolution. By 1838, he had begun helping the Texas navy with the construction of seven ships. Williams and McKinney moved the firm to the island and began promoting the development of Galveston with Michel Menard. Williams would open a bank in Galveston in 1848 and lived in this home until his death.

Letitia Rosenberg Home for Aged Women
1804 Rosenberg Avenue

The Letitia Rosenberg Home for Aged Women was another one of Henry Rosenberg's gifts to the city, following his death in 1893. In 1896, the home was formally dedicated and named in honor of Henry's first wife. The building served as a residence for elderly women in poor health or in need of financial assistance. The three-story building was designed by the famed German architect Alfred Muller in the Victorian Gothic style, with an L-plan configuration to best catch the prevailing southeast breeze and provide views toward the gulf.

Inside, residents could find three deluxe bedroom suites, each with sitting areas and large bathrooms, while a large courtyard is featured in the center of the home. Today, the home sports a theater room and a two-person elevator. This is Muller's largest surviving institutional building. While severely damaged during the 1900 Storm, it was reconstructed and operated as a home for women until 1970.

Chapter 9

ALONG THE SEAWALL

The beaches along the coastline of Galveston Island have always served as a refuge from the heat and the hustle and bustle of everyday life. While this landscape looked different prior to the 1900 Storm, the effect of Galveston's beaches has always been the same: restorative and relaxing. The scene there in September 1900 was anything but. A storm surge higher than a one-story building crashed through the streets and homes of Galveston, destroying as much as it could in its path.

Following the storm, Galveston sought ways to protect itself from further destruction. Civil engineers were brought in, and it was determined that a seawall could afford some protection. Construction began on the Galveston Seawall in September 1902. The initial segment was finished on July 29, 1904, with extensions from 3.3 miles to over 10 miles to follow from 1904 until 1963.

The project did as intended: it protected Galveston and has done so successfully, even taming the destructive force of Ike in 2008 just a little bit. However, it also caused passive erosion in what was once a wide beach with resort businesses constructed right on the sand. Within twenty years, nearly one hundred yards of sand was lost.

Despite this loss of beach, multiple other beaches were added to the coastline, just not as wide and accommodating as before. The beach was different but still a draw, although not enough of one to keep up with the growing population—residential and commercial—in Houston. Galveston, however, remained a popular destination throughout the twentieth century and on into the twenty-first as a draw for tourists to the beaches and the

The Seawall, seen here under construction in July 1905. This shot is looking from the west of Rapid Fire Battery at Fort Crockett. *Courtesy of the U.S. National Archives and Records Administration.*

Strand—and, later, for cruise travelers, who spend a night or two before taking to the open seas. Amusement outlets such as Pleasure Pier, miniature golf, nightclubs (like the Balinese Room), casinos, resorts and more opened up along the Seawall. Today, the seawall and its attractions are as popular as anything along the Strand.

To continue to protect the island, especially following Hurricane Ike, attention has moved beyond one civil engineering feat to another: the Ike Dike. This massive levee system would protect the bay and the industrial facilities that line both the coast and the Houston Ship Channel from a destructive storm. While the idea has gained widespread support from business interests, there is still work to be done, and it is considered to be in a conceptual stage. Further proposals have been added to the project in a variety of ways, one of which includes a proposed lower coastal Lone Star Coastal National Recreation Area. It could be years to decades before anything finally takes shape.

Bath Houses and Boulevard, Galveston, Texas.

Seawall Boulevard, seen here in a postcard from sometime between 1915 and 1924, shows Murdoch's Bathhouse and its neighbor, the Breakers. They were located directly on the beach near the foot of Twenty-Third Street. Bathhouses like these offered bathing suit rentals, changing rooms and shower facilities. The original Murdoch's was destroyed by the 1900 Storm and promptly rebuilt. *Courtesy of the Special Collections, University of Houston.*

Texas Farm-to-Market Road 3005 (or FM 3005) is also known as Seawall Boulevard while it runs along the seawall. The sidewalk adjacent to the boulevard, and located atop the seawall, is claimed to be the longest continuous sidewalk in the world, at 10.3 miles long. Today, the seawall has been listed on the National Register of Historic Places (1977) but also has been designated a National Historic Civil Engineering Landmark by the American Society of Civil Engineers (2001). Huge murals can be found along the seawall, part of a beautification project. These murals were painted by children and showcase the underwater life that thrives in the Gulf of Mexico.

Murdoch's Bathhouse
2219 Seawall Boulevard

A landmark since the late nineteenth century along the beach has been Murdoch's Bathhouse. The original bathhouse opened during the late 1800s and was situated atop the beach near the foot of Twenty-Third Street. Here, beachgoers could rent bathing suits, use a changing room and get showered off. Without any seawall protection, Murdoch's Bathhouse was a casualty of the 1900 Storm.

It didn't take long for proprietor George Murdoch to rebuild. Right on the same site, a new Murdoch's rose to open by February 1901. According to Murdoch, tourist amenities, such as the bathhouses, would be required if Galveston wanted to recover as a destination. Only eight years later, another hurricane struck and destroyed his new bathhouse.

This time, Murdoch rebuilt and reopened in 1911, constructing his operation on wood piles and designing it to withstand hurricanes. His new bathhouse featured 542 rooms, separate changing areas for men and women, a promenade deck for views of the gulf and to host special events and a life-saving station for emergencies. Also inside, allowable with the size of the structure, were independent businesses, including nascent versions of longtime Galveston stalwart Gaido's Restaurant and a gift and souvenir shop operated by William Guyette, whose descendants would later become owners of Murdoch's for several generations.

This improved design and construction proved to be folly, as a few years later, in 1915, a disastrous hurricane struck the island again. Never daunted, Murdoch's rose again like a phoenix. It opened in 1916, this time ten feet above the seawall and expanded to accommodate one thousand bathers. Hurricane Carla knocked it down again in 1961. Again, it came back; this time it lasted until 2008, when Hurricane Ike struck it down. No surprise, it's been rebuilt and thrives with shoppers.

Murdoch's has changed the way it operates due to the needs of island and beach visitors over the years. It's slowly changed from offering bathing suit

This early image of Murdoch's Pier was taken sometime prior to 1919, according to the postage cancellation on this Seawall Specialty Printing postcard. Located near Twenty-Third Street and Seawall Boulevard, this attraction has served beachgoers for more than one hundred years. *Author's collection.*

rentals and changing rooms to refreshments and beach supplies—along with any kind of souvenir you can think of (and many others you never thought you could have).

Sealy House
5310 Seawall Boulevard

Today's Sealy House is hardly what it looked like when it was constructed by Cameron Fairchild in 1931. What was once Fairchild's largest Galveston house has been rehabilitated and incorporated into Landry's Seafood House at the San Luis. This may be for the best, however. The stucco-faced and tile-roofed Mediterranean villa was constructed for George Sealy Jr. and his wife, Eugenia Taylor—one of the very few residences along the beach. For much of its existence, the home actually sat unoccupied and, because of a large stretch of sand, appeared isolated from the seawall since its construction.

The Seawall and Grade Raising Monument
Tremont and Seawall

A pair of Texas granite piers was placed at this location in 1904 to commemorate the completion of the Galveston Seawall and the subsequent grade raising of the island. At the time, this was truly Texas's only coastal city. With little to brag about in the way of design embellishments, it has an amazing stretch of beachfront seagazing to travel down.

Balinese Room Marker
2107 Seawall Boulevard

The famed Balinese Room is gone. Hurricane Ike made sure of that in 2008. The pergola you would once have walked through to enter the boardwalk to the Balinese Room is all that is left. Just to the east of present-day Pleasure Pier, Sicilian immigrant barbers-bootleggers Rosario and Sam Maceo opened a private club located at the end of a very long pier.

The Balinese Room became a hotbed of activity and an elite location during the 1940s and 1950s, and not just for Galvestonians. Entertainment featured in the private club included performances by George Burns, the Marx Brothers,

Here you can see the grade raising, featuring a spouting dredge, that took place following the 1900 Storm. The sidewalk adjacent to Seawall Boulevard, on top of the seawall, is claimed to be the longest continuous sidewalk in the world at 10.3 miles. In 2001, it was designated a National Historic Civil Engineering Landmark. *Courtesy of DeGoyler Library, SMU.*

Sam Maceo's Balinese Room was open during, and after, the Free State of Galveston era. This gambling haven's pier was long enough to allow time for covering up the evidence before police officers could arrive and shut the place down. The Balinese Room was listed on the National Register of Historic Places in 1997 but was destroyed by Hurricane Ike in 2008. Little remains to show its existence today. *Author's collection.*

Bob Hope and even Frank Sinatra along with many other famous acts. Sophie Tucker and Howard Hughes were among its frequent patrons, many ordering a brand-new drink, starting in 1943, called the margarita.

Serving as the headquarters for Maceo's gambling and business empire, the Balinese Room fronted as the finest club and casino in the Southwest. That long pier helped, though. It took so much time for the authorities to move from the entrance along the pier and into the club that by the time they entered, the evidence had been squirreled away. However, after years of trying, the Texas Rangers finally closed the casino during a raid in 1957.

The building, and the fame, lived well beyond its club status. A swanky restaurant was operated here from 1965 until the early 1980s. ZZ Top memorialized the club in lyrics, and *Texas Monthly* called it the Texas nightclub of the century in its December 1999 issue. In 2001, it reopened as a live music club with retail shops and other attractions. Yet Hurricane Ike took it down entirely in the early morning hours of September 13, 2008.

Treasure Isle Motel/Hotel Lucine
1002 Seawall Boulevard

The Treasure Isle Motel was constructed in 1963 by architects Ben J. Kotin and Tibor Beerman. Treasure Island is a great extant example of modern motel design. Kotin, along with his brother Sol, owned the resort, which is where the architect kept his studio. The two-story long, low-slung hotel has undergone a renaissance. Today, it features a modern boutique redesign as Hotel Lucine, with sixty-one rooms and modern ocean-view amenities.

Grand Galvez/Hotel Galvez
2024 Seawall Boulevard

The Hotel Galvez opened in 1911, about the same time that S.G. Gaido opened his sandwich shop at Murdoch's Bathhouse, across the street. Civic leaders had initialized plans for the hotel as far back as 1898, following the destruction by fire of the Beach Hotel. After the destruction of the 1900 Storm, plans for the hotel accelerated, in the hopes that drawing tourists back to the island would help save the future of Galveston. When it opened in June 1911, it was built on the site that once housed the Beach Hotel, the Electric Pavilion and the Pagoda Bathhouse. Designed in a combination

Known now as the Grand Galvez Resort & Spa, the Hotel Galvez, seen here in 1911, sprouted from civic leaders to replace the Beach Hotel, which burned in 1898. Plans accelerated following the 1900 Storm, and it opened in June 1911 at a cost of $1 million. *Courtesy of the Library of Congress.*

of the Mission Revival and Spanish Revival styles by St. Louis architecture firm Mauran, Russell & Crowell, it cost $1 million to complete.

William Moody Jr. purchased the Hotel Galvez in October 1940. It wouldn't be much later, following the entry of the United States into World War II, that the United States Coast Guard would occupy the hotel. From that point forth, for two years, no rooms were rented to tourists. Following the war, however, the Hotel Galvez returned to its role in the local tourist economy. During the 1940s and 1950s, an era of popular illegal gambling in Galveston, the hotel thrived. Famous guests at the Galvez, referred to as the Playground of the Southwest, included Presidents Franklin Roosevelt, Dwight Eisenhower and LBJ. Jimmy Stewart, General Douglas MacArthur, Frank Sinatra and Howard Hughes all checked in at one time or another.

However, once the Texas Rangers put the kibosh on the vice industry in the mid-1950s, the local economy suffered, and the hotel began to deteriorate. In 1965, the hotel underwent major renovations and refurbishing. The Hotel Galvez was bought and sold a few times during the 1970s and underwent an extensive renovation in 1979 following Denton Cooley's purchase of the property. It has since undergone multiple owner changes including Marriott and Wyndham. In 2021, it was purchased and renamed Grand Galvez Resort & Spa. The hotel had been completely renovated by 2023, restoring numerous original features, including the original pink paint scheme on the exterior.

USS *Hatteras*
Off the Coast Shore

The hull of the USS *Hatteras* sits under roughly sixty feet of water and three feet of sand and is located twenty miles off the coast of Galveston. Purchased by the Union navy at the beginning of the Civil War, the USS *Hatteras* was outfitted as a gunboat and assigned to the Union blockade of the ports of the Confederate States of America (CSA). During an engagement with a disguised Confederate raider, the CSS *Alabama*, on the afternoon of January 11, 1863, *Hatteras* was taken by surprise and sunk off the coast of Galveston. The site continues to be monitored to ensure the oil and gas development in the area does not damage the wreckage, which includes *Hatteras*'s steam engine and two iron paddle wheels.

Gaido's Seafood Restaurant
3828 Seawall Boulevard

San Giacinto "S.G." Gaido opened the doors to his sandwich shop at Murdoch's Bathhouse in 1911, selling fresh seafood to beachgoers. By 1920, his sandwich shop had grown into a motel, then a standalone restaurant, becoming Galveston's first seafront restaurant open year-round. Gaido's

Gaido's was founded in 1911 as a sandwich shop at Murdoch's Bathhouse (on Seawall and Twenty-Third Street) by San Giacinto "Cinto" Gaido. Eventually he opened his own brick-and-mortar location, and in the 1920s, Gaido's became the first seafront restaurant to open year-round. *Author's collection.*

original restaurant building was a drive-in that opened in 1936. When S.G. died in 1939, his son and daughter-in-law took over. In 1962, it became one of the first restaurants to be integrated.

Gaido's continues to peel gulf shrimp and shuck Galveston bay oysters by hand, the same way they have for more than a century. Their menu is extensive and, while seafood heavy, has great variety, especially among Southern and Creole recipes. Over more than one hundred years of visitors to Gaido's, seeing someone famous has never been a rare occurrence. Presidents, entertainers and athletes have all enjoyed dinners here, including the esteemed director Alfred Hitchcock. Among those famed diners are those who've held birthday, anniversary and wedding parties at Gaido's. The restaurant continues to be operated within the family. You can't miss the location: look for the giant metal crab and shrimp sculptures rising above the roofline. Right next door are Gaido's Seaside Inn, Nick's Kitchen & Beach Bar.

Fort Crockett/San Luis Resort
5222 Seawall Boulevard

The United States Army Coast Artillery Corps on Galveston Island established a military facility here in the late 1890s. The 1900 Storm disrupted its construction, and the U.S. Army Corps of Engineers spent the next several years rebuilding and expanding the military reservation before it could be re-garrisoned by the U.S. Army. It was named for Tennessee congressman David Crockett, a Texas leader at the Battle of the Alamo.

Once it opened, the facility's first duty was to serve as a mobilization center during the Mexican border troubles in 1912. During the First World War, Fort Crockett served as a United States Army artillery training center. Here, the military would train new troops bound for France in the use of several types of artillery. Prior to the Second World War, Fort Crockett housed the United States Army Air Corps' Third Attack Group, the only group devoted solely to attack aircraft at that time. During the war, the fort served as a German POW camp and was expanded with an additional large gun battery, with focus being placed on defense against German U-boats.

In 1947, following fifty years of service, all harbor defenses were dismantled and the complex was utilized as an army recreation center. On-base offerings included activities such as golf and tennis, while the rest of the island beckoned for entertainment, making the fort's location ideal. Fort

Overlooking the Gulf of Mexico, Fort Crockett served as a defense installation to protect the harbor, city and entrance to the bay. Now managed by the U.S. NOAA National Marine Fisheries Service, the area still contains several historical buildings and fortifications. In the 1980s, the San Luis Resort was built on and behind the battery, incorporating into itself some of the gun emplacements. *Courtesy of Rosenberg Library, Galveston and Texas History Center.*

Crockett was declared surplus in 1953 and released to the General Services Administration for disposal. In the 1950s, the U.S. Fish and Wildlife Service moved in to use the fort as its home for fisheries research. Texas A&M Marine Lab followed in 1958, occupying part of the former army barracks. The largest building at the complex saw renovation in 1963 for occupation by the new Texas A&M Maritime Academy.

On-base, Battery Hoskins, the massive concrete casemates for the guns and magazine, proved uneconomical to remove. These abandoned casemates remained an "abandoned" tourist attraction for decades until the San Luis Resort, Spa & Conference Center was built on and behind the battery. The casements are clear and visible from the seawall—one emplacement now hosts a swimming pool, while the other sports a wedding gazebo. The resort is the biggest hotel on the seawall, standing at fifteen stories and containing more than two hundred rooms and one hundred condominium apartments.

1900 Storm Memorial Statue
4800 Seawall Boulevard

Standing at ten feet in height, this bronze monument to those lost in the 1900 Storm, called *Victims of the Galveston Flood* and created by Florentine

The 1900 Storm memorial statue was created by Galveston sculptor David W. Moore in memory of those who lost their lives in the hurricane. The bronze statue stands ten feet high and was installed on the storm's one-hundredth anniversary in 2000. *Author's collection.*

sculptor Pompeo Coppini, features a mother holding a small child in the middle of the storm with another child on her hip. It was installed on the storm's one-hundredth anniversary in 2000. The full memorial was created by Galveston sculptor David W. Moore, in memory of the more than six thousand men, women and children who died during the disastrous storm. When it struck in September 1900, it carried with it a fifteen-foot storm surge and 134-mile-per-hour winds. When Hurricane Ike struck in 2008, the coastline at Galveston was again laid to waste; however, this statue stood strong. Other works by Coppini on the island include the *Alamo Cenotaph* as well.

Miller's Seawall Grill
1824 Seawall Boulevard

Since 1976, Miller's Seawall Grill has offered up both amazing seafood and southern comfort (and more) recipes as well as some of the best views of the Gulf. Miller's current owners, Donald Clark and David LeBouef, acquired

For nearly fifty years, Miller's Seawall Grill has had one of the best views of any of the restaurants along the Seawall. Housed in one of the more unique buildings along the Boulevard, Miller's is well known for its comfort food and Southern favorites. *Author's collection.*

the restaurant in 2002 and solidified their offerings and recipes before a fire roared through the kitchen on July 17, 2018, forcing the doors closed. Three months later, Miller's reopened, with long lines of customers eager to return. The duo sold the operation to longtime manager Sherry Smith in May 2020. The unique house, somewhat resembling a wooden castle, sits on a tiny triangle all its own along the Seawall.

STEWART BEACH

The idea for Stewart Beach arose from a late 1930s trip that Galveston's mayor Brantley Harris took along the Atlantic coast. There he saw the large public beaches such as Asbury Park, Rockaway Beach and New York's Jones Beach. He also saw an opportunity for Galveston. At that time, the western part of East Beach was owned by the Galveston City Company, and the federal government owned the portion to the east of where Ferry Road and the Seawall cross and out to the jetties. When Harris returned, he persuaded the Galveston City Company to donate its portion of East Beach to the city, and the project met with approval.

The project brought in Houston engineer and architect Robert Cummins to design the plan. Jones Beach former assistant manager Donald Boyce was hired to supervise the construction and manage the site, to be called Stewart Beach Park, after Maco Stewart Sr., Galveston resident, title company founder and one of the largest oil operators in Texas, whose son was one of the shareholders in the Galveston City Company. As the United States was in the depths of the Great Depression, the Roosevelt Administration provided the labor through the Works Progress Administration to build the park.

When Stewart Beach was dedicated on July 18, 1941, visitors found more than just sand and surf; they discovered a new wonderland including a boardwalk, a building hosting a concession stand and restrooms, a gift shop, a beach service office to rent out umbrellas and chairs and cement slabs on either end of the boardwalk—one for dancing and the other for roller skating. That night, big band trumpeter Frankie Littlefield and his orchestra played the park's first of many dances.

Over the years, a variety of activities arrived and faded away. Miniature golf, archery and kiddie amusement rides were all added at one time or another. In 1948, workers uncovered an old military shell road buried under the sand. It was cleared, resurfaced and lengthened and used as an airstrip for brief sightseeing tours over the Gulf. The following year, the Corps of Engineers turned over the remainder of East Beach to the city so that Stewart Beach Park could be expanded.

While the amount of events in Galveston haven't decreased, many have changed. Lost are events like the Pageant of Pulchritude, but swimsuit competitions, like the resurrected Galveston Island Revue Weekend, remain. Shown here is a similar type of competition held on the beach in 1923. *Courtesy of Library of Congress.*

Menard Park Bandstand
2222 Twenty-Eighth Street

Located across from the Seawall and Pleasure Pier is Menard Park, named for town founder Michel Menard. From the Seawall, you can see the rec center building, but travel behind the sea turtle mural and the McGuire Dent Recreation Center building and you will find a playground, splash pad, skate park, dog park and tennis court. Out in front of the rec center, which was built during World War II to serve as a USO building, and right behind that big painted turtle is a stage with an acoustic concrete shell-shaped wall wrapping around it.

Acquired by the city in 1915, this is one of the few green parks in the city. From the early 1930s until the end of segregation, the stretch of beachfront that faces the park was reserved for use by African Americans. During the island's heyday in the 1940s and 1950s, musicians such as Clarence "Gatemouth" Brown, Frank Sinatra and Duke Ellington all graced the stage, which continued to be used consistently through the 1980s. It sat empty and unused following a series of Battle of the Bands concerts in the 1990s; bands began playing again at the bandstand in the 2020s.

Langbehn House
1802 Seawall Boulevard

This, along with the Sealy House up at Fifty-Third and Seawall, is one of the few residential houses standing along the Seawall. Much more modest than its residential neighbor, the Langbehn House was designed and built by shipping agent Fred A. Langbehn. Early twentieth-century photographs show more buildings along the Seawall that are similar, with stucco surfaces and arched verandas, but this is one of the few that remains. When it was constructed in 1915, Langbehn employed the use of deep pile foundations and utilized reinforced concrete in his construction, both of which likely helped it ride out the storm of 1915 unscathed.

Crockett Courts
4214 Avenue U

These gable-roofed, brick-faced tourist courts may be some of the smallest abodes on the island. Facing the back of Fort Crockett, they were erected in 1937, just off the seawall. They are indicative of the type of tourist motor court that sprang up in towns such as Galveston to attract more tourists to their locales. Crockett Court offered up two styles, a two-bay-style home and a stretched three-bay style as well.

Mermaid Pier
2205 Seawall Boulevard

Standing next door to Murdoch's Bathhouse, Mermaid Pier is separated from its neighbor by only 160 feet. Both sites can trace their roots back to 1910 and both, along with the Ocean Grill, sit atop the site of the original Murdoch's Bathhouse, itself destroyed in the 1915 storm, rebuilt and again damaged by Hurricane Carla in 1961. The Little family, who have owned both Murdoch's and Mermaid Pier since 1979, decided to join the two businesses as part of an expansion. The operation added nearly ten thousand square feet of retail space, wheelchair ramps and an open-air deck that connects the two.

Ducky's Beach Marker
5800 Seawall Boulevard

For hundreds of years, people living on the island or visiting it have enjoyed the sandy beaches of Galveston. It's hard to pinpoint exactly or even ballpark the number of people who have either lost their lives in the Gulf waters or been saved from them. One of Galveston's original professional lifeguards was a man named F.M. "Ducky" Prendergast. Ducky has been credited with saving more than four hundred people from drowning in the Galveston surf. He got his start in the 1920s and continued saving lives until his retirement in 1992. From 1951 to 1992, he also owned and operated a popular beach concession business, known as Ducky's Beach, at Fifty-Ninth Street. He passed away in 2002 at the age of ninety-four.

Saint Mary's Orphan Asylum Site
6801 Seawall Boulevard

When the 1900 Storm struck the island, it cared little about economic status, home size, family members, friends, businesses, etc. It swept in and destroyed with no discernment. When it finally passed and the waters receded, more than six thousand men, women and children were dead, among them ten Sisters and ninety children from the St. Mary's Orphans Asylum, operated by the Sisters of Charity. The Sisters came to the island to care for the sick and infirm but found a desperate need for an orphanage in the 1870s following yellow fever epidemics.

The Sisters would move their original orphanage from the hospital location to a site three miles to the west, located on beachfront property—far from town and the threat of yellow fever—on the former estate of Captain Farnifalia Green. That amazing beachfront location, one weekend in September 1900, turned out to be a fateful decision. Early on the morning of September 8, winds swept in from the north and the tides of the southern gulf began rising, sending large waves crashing upon the beach, which only increased as the day progressed until the water began sweeping into residential areas.

The orphanage's two large two-story dormitories sat behind a row of tall sand dunes supported by salt cedar trees. They also had balconies that faced the gulf. The water and winds swept across the island, whittling down the sand dunes until the water swept over them and reached the dorms. The children were moved to the newest building, the girls' wing, as it was considered stronger, where they gathered in the first-floor chapel. As the day progressed, they moved to the second story, then the Sisters had a worker collect clothesline rope. Winds broke one hundred miles per hour around six o'clock, flying debris swirling and cutting down trees, homes, and people. The main tidal surge hit at seven thirty, lifting homes and sending them like battering rams into each other. The first floor of St. Mary's Infirmary filled with water while Sisters pulled refugees out of the water and onto second-story balconies. At the orphanage, the children and Sisters listened as the boy's dormitory collapsed and was carried away by the water.

That clothesline? The Sisters cut it into sections and tied the children to the cinctures they wore around their waists, each Sister tying between six and eight children to herself. Eventually, the girls' dorm was lifted from its foundation as well, the bottom falling out and the roof collapsing, trapping those inside. Only three boys from the orphanage survived; all three were found together in a tree in the water after floating for more than a day. The Sisters and the children tied to them, who perished, were buried where they were found, with the children still attached to them. Two Sisters were found together across the bay on the mainland, one still tightly holding two children in her arms, even in death. A new orphanage was constructed the following year, and St. Mary's Infirmary was repaired. There was still work to do.

Today, the site is marked by a historical marker near Sixty-Ninth Street and Seawall Boulevard. Other than that, you would never know an orphanage once stood there. Today, that marker sits along the Seawall's beach side, across the street from a Walmart Supercenter. St. Mary's Orphan Asylum reopened at Fortieth and Q Streets in 1901, remaining there until it closed in 1967. Today, the building houses the Bryan Museum.

Chapter 10
THE OUTSKIRTS

Developers came to Galveston Island's west end in 1891 with a plan to lay out a new city called South Galveston. While they never came to fruition, construction plans called for city blocks, freshwater ponds, streets, lots for homes, a post office, a large hotel and a racetrack.

Also located on the west side of Galveston Island is the city of Jamaica Beach. The entire island, with the exception of Jamaica Beach, is located within the Galveston city limits. Prior to the development of Jamaica Beach, the area was a burial ground for the Karankawa people. Envisioned as a "weekend playground" with two thousand lots for a resort subdivision close to a marina when it was created in 1956, Jamaica Beach was prosperous from the start.

Included in the founding organization were Jack Valenti, an American political advisor who would serve as a special assistant to LBJ, was the longtime president of the Motion Picture Association America and developed the MPAA film rating system, and Welcome Wilson, who had served in the Eisenhower and Kennedy administrations as a director of the Office of Civil and Defense Mobilization and was a special ambassador to Nicaragua. The prosperous start got a bit of a boost in the 1960s when the discovery of a skull connected to the Karankawas brought additional exposure and led to an increase in visitors. Almost all the lots on Jamaica Beach were sold by the 1970s.

Unfortunately, a decline in the United States economy shortly thereafter caused developers to close their doors due to bankruptcy. The residents who remained pooled resources and skills and formed the foundation of the community that exists today. It was incorporated in 1975 and experienced growth from 141 residents in 1978 to 624 by 1990 and 1,078 by 2020.

Stewart's Mansion
14520 Stewart Road

This Spanish-style house was constructed in 1926 as Isla Ranch, so named by its first owner, George Sealy. The Sealys were a prominent early twentieth century family in Galveston, and George was a financier and a civic leader, eventually serving as president of the Galveston Wharf Company. He publicized the city as the Oleander City, due to his love of flowers, and was among those chiefly responsible for the beautification of both the Broadway and Twenty-Fifth Street esplanades.

The Sealys put the property up for sale in 1933, and it was purchased by Maco Stewart, the founder of what would become Stewart Title Company. In 1944—ironically, the same year that George Sealy passed away—Stewart deeded the house and eleven surrounding acres to the University of Texas Medical Branch. UTMB used it as the residence of the medical branch's dean until 1967, when George Mitchell's development company purchased the home and property.

Laffite's Cove Nature Preserve
3503 Eckert Drive

Galveston Island is a birder's paradise and opportunities to explore are abundant throughout. Laffite's Cove Nature Preserve (LCN) is one of the best and sits on land once inhabited by the Karankawa Indians and later by pirates. The park is so named as this was where the famed pirate Jean Laffite established his pirate outpost between 1817 and 1821. Today, the land serves as an outpost for not a thousand pirates but scores of birds and is maintained by Laffite's Cove Nature Preserve.

As you follow Stewart Road toward the site and once again inside the park, when you turn onto Eckert Drive, you'll want to keep your eyes peeled for waders and waterfowl at the ponds on both sides. The preserve consists of freshwater ponds, grasslands, marshes, an oak woodland, a boardwalk over a large pond, a gazebo, numerous trails and a nature center. From the nature center's parking lot, a good labyrinth of trails affords you the opportunity to spot such birds as the roseate spoonbill, Wilson's snipe, bufflehead, sora, teal and so many more.

Galveston Army Airfield/Scholes International Airport
2115 Terminal Drive

The location of the Galveston International Airport started being used for aircraft operation in the early 1920s. Some of the earliest Texas aircraft operators, like Fen Waters and Bob Scholes, the airport's eventual namesake, began offering rides and aerobatic demonstrations while using East Beach as a runway. Shortly thereafter, they were forced by the city to cease such operations. As a result, Fen Waters was offered the use of what is the present site of the airport by a friend who was operating a watermelon farm and cattle ranch on the property.

It didn't become just a flying field; instead the Galveston Municipal Airport was established in 1931. Then, during World War II, the property was designated a United States Army Air Corps base and dubbed Galveston Army Air Field. Through the work of the Army Corps of Engineers and funds made available by Congress through the Civil Aeronautics Authority three hard-surface runways were constructed to accommodate the army's aircraft for not only training but also watching the skies and waters above the Gulf of Mexico for protection. Following the war, the airfield was deactivated on November 15, 1945, and ownership was transferred back to the City of Galveston.

The terminal building you see today was completed in 1949 and renamed Scholes Field in honor of the airport manager and aviation pioneer mentioned earlier. As late as 1948, it was an active seaplane base. Since opening, it has offered airline services to Houston on Trans-Texas Airways, Braniff and Houston Metro Airlines De Havilland out of Canada, and in the 1980s, it hosted the commuter service of Texas Airlines to Houston's International Airport. Later, it was not uncommon for flights to land at Clear Lake City, near NASA's Johnson Space Center. Additionally, the airport served as home to the Lone Star Flight Museum from 1985 to 2017, when the museum moved inland to Ellington Field.

Today, the airport can accommodate aircraft as large as a Boeing 767, and there is the potential of airline service returning amid the corporate aircraft and oil industry helicopters and airplanes already utilizing the runways. It continues to be a refueling stop for transient military aircraft with the Gulf of Mexico's military operations area and also serves as the destination for air ambulances transferring patients to the island's Shriners Burn Hospital for Children.

Moody Gardens
One Hope Boulevard

The Moody Gardens you see before you today is nothing like what it started out as. Envisioned as an island tourist destination, it started out much smaller. In 1986, Moody Gardens first opened as a horse barn with an adjacent riding arena. Here, Hope Therapy, with funds from the Moody Foundation, provided a hippotherapy riding program for people with head injuries. Additionally, the Hope Arena convention center (now expanded and called the Moody Gardens Convention Center) was established. A couple of years later, Moody Gardens imported white Florida sand to create Palm Beach, and Seaside Safari (known now as the Learning Place) opened. Then the iconic pyramids were added—first the Rainforest Pyramid in 1993, followed by the Discovery Pyramid in 1997 and the Moody Gardens Hotel and Spa, along with the 1.5-million-gallon Aquarium Pyramid, one of the largest of its kind in the world. The complex has continued is expansion with more rooms and an exhibit hall and renovated the Moody Gardens Golf Course.

Edward and Helen Oppenheimer Bird Observatory
13102 Stewart Road

Like the Coastal Heritage Preserve (CHP), the Edward and Helen Oppenheimer Bird Observatory is operated by Artist Boat. It was built to inspire visitors to connect with nature as well as to help protect the disappearing habitat of native plants and animals. While this is Galveston's first public pull-off birding access, the land along Settegast and Stewart Roads has been well-known as a prime birding locale for nearly a century. Free and open to the public, much like the CHP, this land affords you the opportunity to observe wildlife and view what an unblemished Galveston might have looked likes. Amenities to be found here include ADA access, a parking lot, portable restrooms, a 150-foot boardwalk, an observation platform designed by the Gulf Coast Design Lab at the University of Texas at Austin and a bike rack. It is open to the public daily from dawn to dusk.

Galveston Island State Park
14901 FM 3005

Galveston Island State Park protects over two thousand acres of Gulf coastal dunes, wetlands, beaches, brackish ponds and estuaries. Visitors and campers in the state park have access to numerous trails throughout to use for the scenery and wildlife, which includes Kemp's ridley sea turtle. Habitats along these trails include surf, dunes, beach, freshwater ponds, wetlands, bayous, bay shoreline and coastal prairie. While the entire island originally served as home to the indigenous Karankawa and Akokisa peoples, European explorers and pirates would make their presence known from the 1500s to the 1800s. The process of protecting the land, which started in 1950, gave this land to the state to be used and maintained as a preserve and for any other purpose. In 1975, the park finally opened to the public.

Hurricanes and tropical storms remained an issue. In September 1998, Tropical Storm Frances destroyed the park's sand dunes, which were the only protection the park had for its freshwater habitats and visitor facilities. Using recycled Christmas trees to trap and accumulate sand, the dunes were restored. In September 2008, the park was damaged once again, this time by Hurricane Ike. The park reopened for outdoor recreation and camping the following year. The park straddles FM 3005, and newer facilities have been constructed in recent years in order to enhance the experience of all visitors.

San Luis Pass and County Park
14001 CR257 (a.k.a. Blue Water Highway)
Freeport, Texas

San Luis itself was once an island as well, known as Follet's Island and inhabited as early as 1836. In 1878, the United States Life Saving Service Act established a coastal lifesaving station near the strait of San Luis Pass. After seventy years of service here, the station was damaged by a hurricane in 1949; it had discontinued waterborne search and rescue service by 1950. Additionally, Hurricane Ike, in September 2008, drastically affected the topography of the beach. Prior to the storm, a driveway led down to the

Found at the southwestern end of Galveston Island is the 1970 San Luis Pass Bridge. Stretching 1.3 miles long over the San Luis Pass, the "Bluewater Highway's" toll bridge connects Galveston with San Luis Island. Historically, the pass was a popular "back entry" into Galveston Bay for smugglers and pirates. *Author's collection.*

public beach access; both are now part of the Gulf. The land that contained the bait house of the fishing pier that once existed is now submerged.

Located across the strait of water from Galveston Island into Brazoria County is the San Luis Pass-Vacek Toll Bridge. Taking this two-dollar toll bridge will lead you over the San Luis Pass and toward the county park. The San Luis Pass is a strait that connects the waters of West Bay out into the open Gulf of Mexico. On the other side of the bridge sits San Luis Pass County Park. Despite the strait's beauty and beautiful sights, it is an extremely dangerous body of water. Fishermen and swimmers have been taken and killed in the waters of the pass. This is due in large part to the Gulf Stream oceanic currents, widely fluctuating tides (varying by almost two feet in height) and marine sediment.

Calvary Catholic Cemetery
2506 Sixty-Fifth Street

Bishop Nicholas A. Gallagher acquired the land for Calvary Cemetery between 1882 and 1883. The Catholic Cemetery on Avenue K was beginning to fill up, with no room for expansion. The cemetery is entered on the Sixty-Fifth Street side and contains three mortuary vaults. It is surprising that they are still standing despite their exposed setting in the cemetery. While there are many prominent residents here, there are four sites you won't want to miss.

Architect Nicholas J. Clayton designed a High Victorian domed vault for real estate investor Gustav Opperman, who commissioned Clayton to build it for his wife. The vault's cement plaster, designed in the Italian Renaissance style, has been battered and weathered over the past century-plus. The vault is now under the care of the Galveston Historical Foundation.

Across from the Opperman vault sits the burial place of Clayton himself. When he died in 1916, his widow couldn't afford a proper headstone. It took until 1983 for a historian to have the present headstone placed.

Finished in white-painted plaster is the Goggan family vault. Also domed, it is Victorian Gothic in style. It is often attributed to Clayton, as it does resemble his other works and he previously did some work for other Goggan family members. However, this has never been substantiated.

South of the Oppermann and Goggan vaults sits the Societa Italiana di Mutuo Soccorrso, which dates to 1888. A large number of Italian immigrants came to the island in the nineteenth century. In 1876, they formed the Italian Mutual Benevolent Society to provide assistance to immigrants. They also purchased a plot, in 1888, for this mausoleum, also known as the Italian Vault. The vault provides space for twelve crypts, while the outside features Gothic-style designs such as gargoyles, buttresses and Corinthian columns at the entrance.

Rosewood Cemetery
2825 Sixty-Third Street

In 1911, a group of African Americans citizens organized themselves as the Rosewood Cemetery Association. The goal was to designate space exclusively for African Americans, the first on Galveston Island. Previously, African Americans were prevented from interring their dead at nearly every cemetery, save for Lakewood Cemetery's designated area or the New Potters Field on the outskirts of town. in the city. The association identified and purchased its land from Joe Levy's family, dividing up the shares among the twenty-six shareholders, which included churches, associations, individuals and more. Roughly a year later, the first burial, that of the infant Robert Bailey, took place on February 1, 1912.

Over four hundred more burials, primarily from 1914 to 1915, took place before Frank Boyer was laid to rest on June 29, 1944, in the last burial at Rosewood. Interred here are a number of prominent Galvestonians, many leaders in the community, as well as longtime dockworkers, World War I vets and a number of victims of the 1915 hurricane. While 411 graves have been identified and listed in the records, markers exist for only a score of them. The future decades saw a drastic change in the viewscape of this historic cemetery. The construction that began in 1951 resulted in the blocking of Greens Bayou's natural outlet, forcing the water onto the cemetery land and frequently flooding it. Later in the 1950s, additional cemetery land began being gradually sold to developers.

By the end of the twentieth century, very few maps of Galveston even showed Rosewood Cemetery. It was in danger of being lost to the ages. Then, in 2006, the cemetery was donated to the Galveston Historical Foundation as a project of its African American Heritage Committee. A historical marker followed in 2011. Efforts to preserve this crucial Galveston site continue to this day.

Dos Vacas Muertas Bird Sanctuary
Sea Bird Drive

While relatively small compared to other bird sanctuaries, Dos Vacas Muertas is a diverse ecological system. You'll find a small spartina marsh, coastal grassland with cord grass, a pond lined with cane, and a wood lot filled with live oaks. This variety of habitats has resulted in a year-round display of birds. Once the location of a dream home for Dr. George Clayton and his wife, Jane, it was destroyed during Hurricane Alicia. The Claytons chose a different locale to rebuild and instead began restoring the pond, trees, fence, oleanders and salt cedars while adding more foliage. They jokingly named the property Dos Vacas Muertas, Spanish for "two dead cows." Around 2001, the Claytons donated the property to the Houston Audubon Society in order for Dos Vacas Muertas to remain a bird sanctuary in perpetuity. Today, the wooded and secluded sanctuary is considered one of the top bird sanctuaries in the state. The six-acre site is free and open to the public from dawn until dusk.

Artist Boat Coastal Heritage Preserve
13117 Settegast Road

Onc of the largest undeveloped areas in Galveston is the Coastal Heritage Preserve. Covering 898 acres, this conservation area is a good place to see what Galveston Island looked like when explorers and Anglo-American settlers first appeared. Here you will find grassy fields, wide-open spaces, abundant wildlife and bountiful bays. The primary goal of Artist Boat, founded in 2008, is to preserve and restore 1,400 contiguous acres from the bay to the beach. This will allow for public access to view barrier island habitats and serve as a regional amenity for the public to connect with Galveston Bay's ecosystem. Access is available via certain activities such as public kayak adventures and volunteer workdays, so make sure to call ahead before visiting.

Karankawa Campsite
16721 Jolly Roger Road
Jamaica Beach, Texas

While there isn't much history to see aboveground here other than a Texas Historical Commission marker, this site dates to well before Europeans arrived on the island. While now extinct, the nomadic Karankawa Indians lived all along the Texas coast, using the Gulf's resources for their survival. This specific location is one of several known Karankawa campsites or burial sites. When Spanish explorers under Cabeza de Vaca arrived in the area in 1528, the Karankawa aided them. However, following the French expedition of Réne-Robert Cavelier, Sieur de La Salle, in 1685, they resisted all intruders. As time wore on and more people arrived on the island, the tribe began to evaporate due to the introduction of new diseases but also through battles with Anglo-American settlers and Jean Laffite's pirates. The Karankawa were known for their exceptional archery skills, their ferocious appearance and their height (between six and seven feet tall), and they were alleged to have practiced ceremonial cannibalism. By the 1840s, the Karankawa of Texas had virtually disappeared. This campsite was discovered in 1962. Today, the site has been developed for residents to use as the Jamaica Beach City Park.

The Kettle House
14106 Miramar Drive

One of the most unique properties you can find in Galveston is the Kettle House. While it is privately owned, visitors can go onto any number of short-term rental websites to rent this spherical home. The round steel building with its shingled roof, sitting on a grassy lot, can easily be seen on the north side of Termini–San Luis Pass Road, as you head toward San Luis Pass.

For decades, this structure was a fixture among the island's unusual and mysterious locations. Back in the 1960s, Alabama-born World War II vet Clayton Stokley created the "Kettle House." At the time, Stokley worked for Graver Tank & Manufacturing Co. Inc. The company would sell steel to its employees at cost, and Stokley had an entrepreneurial spirit, constructing various commercial spaces he intended to operate. After opening a nightclub, a couple of convenience stores and a liquor store in the Houston area, Stokley turned his sights to Galveston for his next venture, a retail outlet.

The Kettle House, located on the far west end of Galveston, is a short walk from the coastline. The area is prone to hurricanes, and this tiny metal house with sloping walls stands as an anomaly among its stilted neighbors. Squat and sturdy, it survived Hurricane Ike and other weather conditions that have destroyed many others. It has stood here since its construction by Clayton Stokley more than fifty years ago. *Author's collection.*

Around the same time, a client had the company craft a unique sphere made of three-eighths-inch-thick steel. When the deal fell through and the company was left with a giant hollow steel ball. Stokley saw it as an opportunity. He and his friends and family broke down the structure into parts and then shipped it to Galveston, working throughout the weekends to construct the building themselves. Unfortunately, Stokley's plans never materialized. Soon after the exterior was finished, he suffered a stroke, then died in 2005.

The home was willed to Mary Etheridge-Rachels, Stokely's daughter. She did what she could to maintain and improve the home. Soon after, however, her husband was diagnosed with cancer, and after a twelve-year fight with myeloma, he passed away. Michael and Ashely Cordray of Save 100 purchased the structure, renovating it for the show *Big Texas Fix* and opening it up to the public for short-term rentals.

Chapter 11
PELICAN ISLAND AND BEYOND

Linked to Galveston Island by a causeway, Pelican Island is home to the Texas A&M University at Galveston and two museum ships, along with a smattering of other interesting pieces from other ships such as the USS *Texas*, the USS *Carp* and the USS *Tautog*. Seawolf Parkway—the original name of the Galveston Naval Museum was Seawolf Park—is the only street that runs across the island. The Intracoastal Waterway borders it to the north, separating Pelican Island from another island.

Pelican Island sits directly north of the Galveston Harbor docks, providing protection for the harbor from Galveston Bay and to the ship channel leading to the wharf area. During the Civil War, in 1861, the Confederacy built a small fort on the island with fake cannons, known as "quakers," installed. Following the recapture of Galveston by John Bankhead Magruder in 1863, the Union placed six casement guns on the island and eight more at Fort Point on Galveston Island, in order to secure the channel for the remainder of the conflict.

Over the years, the island has been used for a variety of businesses. Pelican Island has hosted fish and oyster businesses, an immigration station, a lifesaving station and the Todd Ship Yards. Galveston established the park here in 1955–56 and opened a viaduct in 1958. The commercial and industrial development on the island never met early expectations, and it became an ideal location for the permanent site of Texas A&M University at Galveston.

In 1933, at the peak of the Great Depression, Bolivar Point Lighthouse was declared obsolete and its light extinguished later that year. Over the years, it was battered by multiple hurricanes and accidental shelling from nearby Fort San Jacinto, and Hurricane Ike ripped its finial off and knocked it into the marsh. Since that time, it has been privately owned and is now undergoing the process of restoring the historic structure. *Author's collection.*

Across the harbor is the Bolivar Peninsula. Once you've crossed over on the ferry, which is currently the only way east off the island, you'll arrive at a long spit of land that will lead you to the mainland. Here you will find the remains of Fort Travis and the Bolivar Point Lighthouse, currently under restoration. Keep heading west, and eventually, Beaumont will welcome you.

Galveston Causeway
Interstate 45, Galveston

The original Galveston-Houston causeway was constructed in 1912, spanning Galveston Bay and the Gulf Intracoastal Waterway. The intent was for the path to carry both rail and auto traffic. When a new causeway was constructed to the west in 1939, the original bridge was left for rail traffic. The original bridge remains in use to this day and is now listed on the National Register of Historic Places. Known today as the George and Cynthia Mitchell Memorial Causeway, these two routes carry the

Seen here in 1915, the Galveston-Houston Electric Railway served as an interurban railway between the two cities from 1911 to 1936. It ran fifty miles from downtown Houston to downtown Galveston, making the trip in as little as seventy-five minutes. *Courtesy of the Special Collections, University of Houston Libraries.*

southbound and northbound traffic of I-45 and serve as the main roadway access point to Galveston Island, the second being the Bolivar Ferry.

In September 2008, the causeway flooded badly prior to the landfall of Hurricane Ike. A tremendous storm surge, created by the wide storm, closed traffic to the bridge. This same storm delayed construction of replacement bridges as well. Construction began for both auto routes in 2003, with the northbound route completed in 2005. The southbound route began in 2006 and wasn't finished until November 2008. Additionally, the original drawspan was replaced in 1987 and again in 2012.

Seawolf Park/Galveston Naval Museum
100 Seawolf Park Boulevard

Following World War II, Congress decreed that each state would create a memorial park to one of the U.S. Navy submarines lost during the war. Texas chose a site on Pelican Island. In 1971, the Gato-class submarine USS *Cavalla* (SS-244) was transferred from the navy and towed to the park, which itself was named after the submarine USS *Seawolf* (SS-197), which was last

Seawolf Park is located on Galveston's Pelican Island, a former immigration station site. Today the park offers a popular fishing pier and is home to the Galveston Naval Museum, which highlights the WWII submarine USS *Cavalla* and the USS *Stewart*. The SS *Selma* can be seen at the end of the island. *Author's collection.*

in the Pacific during the war. Seawolf Park is unique in that it features a submarine, the remains of a merchant ship and a destroyer escort designed for antisubmarine warfare, putting the hunter, the hunted and the protector all in the same area. Also in this area of the island is a picnic area, pier fishing locations and shoreline fishing.

USS *Cavalla*
Seawolf Park

This Gato-class submarine was best known for sinking the Japanese aircraft carrier *Shokaku*. Departing New London in April 1944, it arrived at Pearl Harbor in early May before being put to sea on active service. It fought primarily in the eastern Philippines, and the South China and Java Seas. It contributed to the U.S. victory in the Battle of the Philippine Sea, more commonly known as the Marianas Turkey Shoot, and at Peleliu. It was decommissioned and struck from the naval record in 1969 before becoming located on Pelican Island for tours.

USS *Stewart*
Seawolf Park

The Edsall-class destroyer escort USS *Stewart* was named for Rear Admiral Charles Stewart, who commanded the USS *Constitution* during the War of 1812. It is one of only two preserved destroyer escorts in the United States and the only Edsall-class vessel to be preserved. The third ship so named, it was laid down at Houston in July 1942 and commissioned in May 1943 before getting underway for sites along the U.S. Eastern Seaboard and in the Atlantic. In 1945, it transferred to the Pacific, reached Pearl Harbor that summer to conduct additional training before returning to the East Coast and reporting for duty to the Atlantic Reserve Fleet at Philadelphia. In 1974, following its name being struck from the navy list in 1972, it was donated to the City of Galveston. In addition to the ship itself, its propellers were removed and resituated in the park, so visitors could observe them fully.

USS *Carp, Tautog* and *Texas*
Seawolf Park

Also preserved at the park are a few other pieces of other ships. Visitors can see the conning tower of the Balao-class submarine USS *Carp* (SS-338), the sail of the Sturgeon-class nuclear attack submarine USS *Tautog* (SSN-639) and guns from the battleship USS *Texas*.

The *Carp*'s first, and only, war patrol came from June 8 to August 7, 1945, when it cruised off the coast of Honshu, destroying small craft and patrolling for striking carriers. It also served in the Korean War and conducted training and services through 1967 before being decommissioned in 1968 and sold for scrap in 1973. The conning tower remains.

The *Tautog* was in service from August 1968 to March 1997. Most of its training took place in the Pacific, especially in Hawaii, China and Japan, and it later saw service as far north as the North Pole and during the 1977 Uganda crisis. In 1970, it was patrolling the North Pacific Ocean on the Soviet Union's Kamchatka Peninsula, a major base for missile-armed subs of the Soviet navy located at Petropavlovsk-Kamchatsky. While there, *Tautog* was attempting to trail K-108, a Soviet navy submarine, when the two collided. No casualties occurred, but it wasn't until after the Cold War that it was revealed that the K-108 had not broken apart and sunk, as thought at the time, but had been able to return. When *Tautog* arrived in Pearl Harbor, a large portion of one of the K-108's screws was found embedded in its sail, which is on display here. Later excursions and duties included tours in both the Atlantic and Pacific Oceans as well as during the Uganda crisis in 1977.

Behind the USS *Stewart*'s removed propellers are two thirty-inch, fifty-caliber memorial guns. The *Stewart*, famed for its extensive service, primarily during World Wars I and II, these guns were donated from the battleship USS *Texas*, most recently located in La Porte and removed for extensive repairs in Galveston. There is speculation that one such option for USS *Texas*'s permanent rehousing would be somewhere in Galveston.

Texas A&M University at Galveston
200 Seawolf Parkway

In 1965, Galveston businessman George Mitchell purchased a large tract of land on the island, donating some of it for the new permanent home of Texas A&M University at Galveston. The Galveston satellite location began in 1962, serving as a marine laboratory and as the home of what is now the Texas A&M Maritime Academy. The federal government donated the first training ship, the *Texas Clipper*, in 1965. With Mitchell's donation of land, the campus was expanded by one hundred acres and again with an additional thirty-five acres in 1993. Academics at the campus have been distinctly focused on the ocean in the fields of marine biology, marine sciences, oceanography, administration and engineering.

SS *Selma*
Northeast of Galveston Island, Off the Point of Pelican Island

During World War I, the United States faced steel shortages. In response to this and to a burgeoning concern that the mainland of the United States remained vulnerable to attack, President Woodrow Wilson approved the construction of twenty-four concrete vessels. Of these, only half were actually completed. This one, the oil tanker SS *Selma*, was built by F.F. Ley and Company out of Mobile, Alabama, in 1919. It is the only permanent, and prominent, wreck along the Houston Ship Channel and is located directly off Pelican Island, along the route of the Galveston-Bolivar Ferry.

The SS *Selma* was an oil tanker built in 1919 in Mobile, Alabama. One of twelve concrete vessels completed for use during World War I, SS *Selma* is the only permanent, and prominent, wreck along the Houston Ship Channel. It was never put into service during World War I, served as an oil tanker in the Gulf and hit a jetty in Mexico, on which it was placed near Pelican Island, where it still resides. *Author's collection.*

Named to honor the city of Selma, Alabama, for its successful wartime Liberty loan drive, the SS *Selma* was launched on the same day Germany signed the Treaty of Versailles: June 28, 1919. Due to this timing, the 7,500-ton concrete ship never served during the war, instead being placed into service as an oil tanker in the Gulf of Mexico. In May 1920, the *Selma* hit a jetty in Tampico, Mexico. The collision ripped a massive hole in its hull, and repairs were not successful. When attempts to sell the ship also failed, the United States decided to intentionally scuttle the ship. A 1,500-foot-long channel was dug twenty-five feet deep, just off Pelican Island's eastern shoreline. On March 9, 1922, the *Selma* was laid to rest, and there it has remained since. It has been on the National Register of Historic Places since 1994, and ownership of the *Selma* lies in private hands.

Fort Point/Fort San Jacinto
2 Seawall Boulevard

Like Fort Travis, on the other side at Port Bolivar, this site was first reserved for public purposes by the Republic of Texas in 1836. This northeastern tip of the island has seen defense fortifications here since that time. Crude Spanish and French fortifications between 1816 and 1818 actually preceded these, eventually giving way to the small sand forts and batteries that the republic constructed from 1836 to 1844.

Early in the war, Confederate troops pulled down the Bolivar Lighthouse, on the opposite shore, in order to keep Union forces from utilizing it as a shoreline marker. Then, in 1863, the Confederate army constructed Fort Point. An earthen battery was erected with adjacent breastworks out of sandbags. All traces of these early fortifications have since been destroyed, if not by the frequent hurricanes, then at least by the ever-present tides and strong winds that regularly transform the sandy tip of Galveston Island.

The United States Army utilized the location in 1897, around the same time as the construction of Fort Travis. A more substantial fortification was built here, termed Fort San Jacinto, containing three-gun batteries and a direction-finder control station. Like Fort Travis, it didn't last long. Both forts were partially destroyed during the 1900 storm, taking years to rebuild.

The seawall was extended northward in 1921 to protect the area, and the fort was rebuilt. When the Second World War came, new gun emplacements were added for the defense of Galveston. The guns here were manned by both the 265th Coast Artillery and the Twentieth Coast Artillery. Following

Fort San Jacinto, formerly a U.S. coastal defense fortification, was constructed in 1898 at the eastern end of Galveston Island. It was expanded in 1901 and became the first headquarters for Galveston's harbor defenses, sporting three-gun batteries and a direction-finder control station. Only the foundations of these exist today. *Author's collection.*

the war, the reservation was maintained by the Coast Guard as an electronic repair shop. While it was decommissioned in 1959, in 1986, the site was used by the United States Army Corps of Engineers, which was dredging silt from the ship channel. Remaining today is the round, concrete base of one of those 90 mm gun emplacements.

Galveston–Port Bolivar Ferry
1000 Ferry Road
Galveston, Texas

123 SH 87
Port Bolivar, Texas

The Galveston–Port Bolivar Ferry is a free service for all those wishing to enter and leave the island via Highway 87 and has been since 1934. There are three routes on and off the island: one is all the way at the western end of the island at San Luis Pass, and the two major routes, the causeway and

The Galveston–Port Bolivar ferry service provides free transportation between the island and the Bolivar Peninsula. One vessel is in operation twenty-four hours a day, with a second placed in service in the morning. As many as five might be operating at any given time during the summer and holiday seasons. It is not uncommon to see freighters, shrimpers and dolphins nearby. *Author's collection.*

the Galveston–Port Bolivar Ferry, are located on the northeastern tip of the island. The trip covers about 2.7 miles, taking about eighteen minutes to cross from point to point. Each of the ferry boats can carry roughly seventy vehicles and five hundred passengers, and you can drive on and cross to the other side or walk on as a sightseeing expedition. While the service operates twenty-four hours a day, the number of ferries may vary depending on traffic and peak periods; as few as one and as many as six may operate at any given time. Along the way, you get to see Fort Travis, the Bolivar Lighthouse, Seawolf Park, the Galveston skyline, the Galveston Yacht Basin and the many tankers and/or ships anchored or traveling into port or out to sea. Keen eyes will also be able to spot dolphins (and maybe a manatee) leading tankers and shrimp boats as they cut across the water.

Port Bolivar Lighthouse
419 Everett Road
Point Bolivar, Texas

This historic lighthouse served this passage for sixty-one years. The current lighthouse here was built in 1872, replacing a cast-iron lighthouse built in 1852. The first, made at the Baltimore foundry of Murray and Hazlehurst, was pulled down by Confederate troops during the Civil War so that Union warships couldn't utilize it as a navigational aid. When this one was erected as a replacement, it served until being replaced by a different light in 1933.

This brick lighthouse, covered with cast-iron sheets, stands at 116 feet tall and was built by the Bureau of Lighthouses. Originally colored, following 150 years of erosion, it has rusted to a dark brown. During the Galveston Hurricane of 1900, the lighthouse served as a lifesaving shelter for at least 125 people, many of whom had waded through waist-deep water to escape the storm surge that engulfed their human chain of safety.

The lighthouse survived another hurricane in 1915, when winds of 126 miles per hour were recorded. However, the light was knocked out when the storm destroyed the oil house, and it remained dark for two nights. During

The Bolivar Point Lighthouse is one of the few nineteenth-century lighthouses remaining on the Gulf Coast and one of two iron lighthouses in Texas. Constructed in 1872, it operated from November 19, 1872, until it was retired from service on May 29, 1933, shining its light every night during its sixty years—except for two nights during the 1915 Hurricane, which destroyed the oil house. *Courtesy of the United States Coast Guard.*

the storm, the top swayed twelve inches from side to side. This time, sixty-one people took refuge within its walls.

From the 1890s until 1942, the line's closing, the lighthouse looked down on the Gulf, Colorado & Santa Fe Railway. On November 15, 1917, the lighthouse was accidentally shelled by artillery fired from Fort San Jacinto—again, it survived. In 1935, the War Department took possession of the lighthouse. After the war, it was transferred to the War Assets Administration, then sold to a private rancher. Hurricane Alecia hit it in 1983, and Hurricane Ike struck in 2008, ripping the finial off the top and plunging it into the marsh and wiping out the brick kerosene house and additional buildings on the ground. It is temporarily closed to the public, with repair and restoration plans underway through the Bolivar Point Lighthouse Foundation.

Fort Travis Seashore Park
900 State Highway 87
Port Bolivar, Texas

This sixty-acre military site with bunkers is located on the extreme west side of Bolivar Peninsula and within sight of the Bolivar Lighthouse. This location has been a popular one for fortifications throughout the recorded history of Galveston Island. Today, this site is on the National Register of Historic Places and also is a popular park under the jurisdiction of the Galveston County Department of Parks and Cultural Services, containing amenities such as cabanas, camping areas, covered picnic spots and three wetland overlooks.

While this was likely not the first use of this point as a fortification, Mexican manuscripts from 1816 show the location of *campamentos* by Henry Perry and Jean Joseph Amable Humbert, with earthworks built here that same year by Francisco Xavier Mina. Then, in 1819, an attempt was made by Dr. James Long and three hundred men to liberate Spanish Texas. Before proceeding inland with his plan, he established Fort Las Casas, a series of fortifications, in August 1819. During the winter of 1820–21, Long's wife, Jane Herbert Wilkinson Long, remained behind with one child and one servant, reluctant to leave even after learning of her husband's death. Giving birth to a daughter during this period, she earned the nickname "Mother of Texas." This site would become the Republic of Texas's first established fort, constructed to protect the Galveston harbor entrance. This strategic location would help protect the new republic's coastline and immediate

After serving and protecting the coastline since 1899 and through World Wars I and II, Fort Travis has since been repurposed into a waterfront park. It could hold up to 2,500 troops and several types of guns, from rifles to antiaircraft. Barracks and other structures have remained intact and accessible (mostly) to exploration. *Author's collection.*

interior. Using army recruits and slave labor, the republic built an octagonal earth-and-timber fortification. Soon after, in 1838, Samuel D. Parr started the nearby settlement that would become Port Bolivar.

Construction at this site of a more permanent fortification commenced on April 8, 1898, when construction of Fort Travis began. Completed in October 1899, the fort was named in honor of William B. Travis. In 1898, Batteries Ernest and Davis were completed. Battery Kimball followed in 1925 and Battery No. 236 in 1943. Throughout the years, armaments at the site included two twelve-inch guns on barbette carriages, three-inch rapid-fire guns, two eight-inch disappearing guns, three pedestal guns and twelve-inch guns with a range of seventeen miles. Battery 236 was added for World War II and contained two six-inch guns within a casement that included a power plant, magazines, fire control, mess hall and crew quarters. As many as 2,500 troops were stationed at Fort Travis during World War II, when it also served as an internment camp for several German prisoners of war.

Following the 1900 Storm, a seventeen-foot wall was constructed on the south side of the island to serve as a barrier against future storm surge. This seawall extended all the way to the eastern end of the island. The installation was declared surplus in 1949 and, as such, was sold. In 1973, the Galveston County Commissioners Court purchased the site for use as a public park.

BIBLIOGRAPHY

Books

Abbott, Olyve Hallmark. *Texas Ghosts: Galveston, Houston, and Vicinity*. Atglen, PA: Schiffer, 2010.

Alexander, Denise. *Galveston's Historic Downtown and Strand District*. Charleston, SC: Arcadia Publishing, 2010.

Alexander, Drury Blake. *Texas Home of the Nineteenth Century*. Austin: University of Texas Press, 1966.

Anderson, James F. *Galveston Burning: A History of the Fire Department and Major Conflagrations*. Charleston, SC: The History Press, 2021.

Andrews, Michael. *Historic Texas Courthouses*. Houston: Bright Sky Press, 2006.

Baker, Eugene C., ed. *History of Texas and Texans*. Vol. 3. Chicago: American Historical Society, 1914.

Barnstone, Howard. *The Galveston That Was*. College Station, TX: TAMU Press, 2014.

Beasley, Ellen, and Stephen Fox. *Galveston Architecture Guidebook*. Galveston, TX: Galveston Historical Foundation, 1996,

Bixel, Patricia Bellis. *Galveston and the 1900 Storm: Catastrophe and Catalyst*. Austin: University of Texas Press, 2013.

Boatman, T. Nicole. *Galveston's Maceo Family Empire: Bootlegging & the Balinese Room*. Charleston, SC: The History Press, 2014.

Boudreaux, Tommie D., and Alice M. Gatson. *African Americans of Galveston*. Charleston, SC: Arcadia Publishing, 2013.

Cartwright, Gary. *Galveston: A History of the Island by Gary Cartwright*. Fort Worth, TX: Texas Christian University Press, 1998.

Ching, Francis D.K. *A Visual Dictionary of Architecture*. New York: John Wiley & Sons, 1995.

Davis, Brian M. *Lost Galveston*. Postcards of America series. Charleston, SC: Arcadia Publishing, 2010.

Echols, Gordon. *Early Texas Architecture*. Fort Worth, TX: Texas Christian University Press, 2000.

Farrar, R.M. *Buffalo Bayou and the Houston Ship Channel, 1820–1926*. Houston: Chamber of Commerce, 1926.

Fire Museum of Houston and Tristan Smith. *Houston Fire Department*. Charleston, SC: Arcadia Publishing, 2015.

Fountain, Kimber. *Galveston's Red Light District: A History of the Line*. Charleston, SC: The History Press, 2018.

———. *Galveston Seawall Chronicles*. Charleston, SC: The History Press, 2017.

———. *The Maceos and the Free State of Galveston: An Authorized History*. Charleston, SC: Arcadia Publishing, 2014.

Frazier, Donald S. *Cottonclads!: The Battle of Galveston and the Defense of the Texas Coast*. Austin, TX: State House Press, 1998.

Gaido's Seafood Restaurant. *Gaido's Famous Seafood Restaurant: A Cookbook Celebrating 100 Years*. Nashville, TN: Favorite Recipes Press, 2010.

Goeldner, Paul. *Historic American Buildings Survey, Texas Catalog*. San Antonio, TX: Trinity University Press, 1993.

Harris, Cyril. *Dictionary of Architecture and Construction*. New York: McGraw-Hill, 2006.

Henry, Jay C. *Architecture in Texas: 1895–1945*. Austin, TX: University of Texas Press, 1993.

Johnson, Jan. *Yellow Fever on Galveston Island*. Charleston, SC: The History Press, 2022.

Johnston, Marguerite. *Houston: The Unknown City, 1836–1946*. College Station, TX: Texas A&M University Press, 1991.

Jones, W. Dwayne, and Jami Durham. *Galveston: Playground of the Southwest*. Charleston, SC: Arcadia Publishing, 2013.

Kelsey, Mavis P., and Donald Dyal. *The Courthouses of Texas*. College Station, TX: Texas A&M University Press, 2007.

Larson, Erik. *Isaac's Storm: A Man, a Time, and the Deadliest Hurricane in History*. New York: Vintage Publishing, 2000.

Lewis, Ella. *Lost Restaurants of Galveston's African American Community*. Charleston, SC: The History Press, 2021.

Longstreth, Richard. *The Buildings of Main Street: A Guide to American Commercial Architecture*. Walnut Creek, CA: AltaMira Press, 2000.

Maca, Kathleen. *Ghosts of Galveston*. Charleston, SC: The History Press, 2016.

———. *A History of the Hotel Galvez*. Charleston, SC: The History Press, 2021.

Marinbach, Bernard. *Galveston: Ellis Island of the West*. Albany, NY: State University of New York Press, 1984.

McComb, David. *Galveston: A History and a Guide by David McComb*. Austin, TX: Texas State Historical Association, 2015.

Pellerin, Joseph R. *Galveston's Tree Carvings*. Charleston, SC: Arcadia Publishing, 2015.

Poppeliers, J.C. *What Style Is It? A Guide to American Architecture*. Washington, D.C.: Preservation Press, 1983.

Roker, Al. *The Storm of the Century: Tragedy, Heroism, Survival, and the Epic True Story of America's Deadliest Natural Disaster: The Great Gulf Hurricane of 1900*. New York: HarperCollins Publishers, 2015.

Sallee, Alvin L. *Galveston Wharf Stories: Characters, Captains & Cruises*. Galveston, TX: Self-published, 2018.

Schmidt, James M. *Galveston and the Civil War: An Island City in the Maelstrom*. Charleston, SC: Arcadia Publishing, 2021.

Sibley, Marilyn McAdams. *The Port of Houston: A History*. Austin, TX: University of Texas Press, 1968.

Tyler, Ron, Douglas Barnett and Roy R. Barkley, eds. *The New Handbook of Texas*. Austin, TX: Texas State Historical Association, 1996.

Voss, Kurt D. *Galveston's the* Elissa*: The Tall Ship of Texas*. Charleston, SC: Arcadia Publishing, 2009.

Weincek, Henry. *The Moodys of Galveston and Their Mansion*. College Station, TX: TAMU Press, 2010.

Whiffen, Marcus. *American Architecture Since 1780: A Guide to the Styles*. Cambridge, MA: MIT Press, 1969.

Willett, Donald. *Galveston Chronicles: The Queen City of the Gulf*. Charleston, SC: The History Press, 2013.

Withey, Henry F., and Elsie Rathburn. *Biographical Dictionary of American Architects: Deceased*. Los Angeles, CA: Hennessey and Ingalls, 1970.

Wooten, Heather Green. *Old Red: Pioneering Medical Education in Texas*. Austin, TX: Texas State Historical Association, 2013

Wright-Gidley, Jodi, and Jennifer Marines. *Galveston: A City on Stilts*. Charleston, SC: Arcadia Publishing, 2008.

Young, Samuel Oliver. *A Thumbnail History of the City of Houston, Texas: 1836–1912*. Houston: Rein & Son, 1912.

Other Publications

Bryant, Keith L., Jr. "Railway Stations of Texas: A Disappearing Architectural Heritage." *Southwestern Historical Quarterly* 79, no. 4 (April 1976): 417–40.

Smith, Frank P. "A Detailed Description of the Port." In *Houston Port Book*, 19–21. N.p., 1935.

Other Print Sources

I also utilized the Department of the Interior's resources for locations listed on the National Register of Historic Places. These documents provide information on the past and present history of historic locations throughout Houston via applications filed with these departments for inclusion on said lists. By visiting the Texas Historical Commission's Atlas website: https://www.thc.texas.gov/preserve/projects-and-programs/national-register-historic-places, a listing of every document utilized can be found at: United States Department of the Interior. National Register of Historic Places Nomination Forms, City: Galveston.

ABOUT THE AUTHOR

Tristan Smith is an independent historian living in Houston, Texas. He has worked for museums and nonprofits in Kansas, Missouri and Texas for over twenty years in marketing, curation, education, volunteer, management and administrative capacities. Museums he's been involved with have featured natural history, the 1950s, fine art, community history, a sunken steamboat found in a Kansas cornfield, a United States president, firefighting history and photography. He has also consulted organizations and municipalities in historic preservation. He is the author of *Houston Fire Department* (Images of America series, Arcadia Publishing, 2015), *A History Lover's Guide to Houston* (The History Press, 2020) and *Historic Cemeteries of Houston and Galveston* (The History Press, 2023). His writing can also be found in *Authentic Texas* magazine, and additional work can be found on his website, www.thehistorysmith.com.

Visit us at
www.historypress.com